The Lost Secret of Immortality

Published by
Golden Elixir Productions LLC
PO Box 3240
Ashland OR 97520
www.lostsecretofimmortality.com

All translations of *Tao Te Ching*© by Solala Towler

Cover Design: Nancy Hutchison
Illustration: And, Inc.

The Lost Secret of Immortality

by Barclay Powers

Table of Contents

Foreword

Chapter One. Saintly Deaths and Disappearing Bodies......................4

Chapter Two. Beginning with the Body...11

Chapter Three. The Human Mind – Science or Illusion....................15

Chapter Four. Splitting Spirit and Science.......................................19

Chapter Five. Three Bodies: The Trikaya of Buddhism...................25

Chapter Six. Rocks Can Change Your Mind....................................34

Chapter Seven.The Philosopher's Stone...41

Chapter Eight. Kundalini..50

Chapter Nine. Mysteries of the Void..58

Chapter Ten. An Experiential Interlude of the Real Now.................65

Chapter Eleven. The Six Yogas of Naropa.......................................69

Chapter Twelve. Shamanism...90

Chapter Thirteen. Patterns, Energy and the Flow in the Universe..100

Chapter Fourteen. The Three Treasures and the Golden Embryo...115

Chapter Fifteen. Sacred Union: Sexual Yoga.................................139

Chapter Sixteen. Chinese Medicine..156

Chapter Seventeen. What is Real Kung Fu?...................................169

Chapter Eighteen. Science Rediscovers The Philosopher's Stone..180

Chapter Nineteen. In Conclusion..194

Biblography...201

FOREWORD

In the 21st century it has become possible for all individuals to achieve complete inner illumination through their own self-cultivation by using methods and information which have long been hidden but are now available to all. It is this inner illumination which represents the eternal quest for ultimate truth of both science and religion. The source of each human being's consciousness is this primordial freedom of complete enlightenment, and it is this awareness, which is eternally present, that represents the true union of the human body, soul and spirit.

This book represents a revolution in consciousness as well as the rediscovery of the most ancient truths of both science and religion. These truths are coupled with the premise that the complete evolution of mind and body is actually the ultimate goal of individual freedom, which is the origin of Western science, Chinese medicine and Indian spirituality.

Science has actually rediscovered the source of itself, the legendary Philosopher's Stone; whether the starting point of the body is called the Golden Embryo in Chinese alchemy, the Kundalini in Indian yoga or the Original Face in Zen Buddhism, true freedom has always been the Elixir of Immortality. The reader will discover that the possibility of attaining the Rainbow Body – the dissolution of the body at death–represents the completion stage of real meditation and the complete evolution of the human mind/body continuum.

It is possible for all human beings to achieve complete enlightenment through the variety of methods outlined in this book, which include sexual yoga, breathing practices, and many other techniques that seek to activate and harness the original pre-birth enlightened energy of the body.

This book is the first scientific explanation of the goal of meditation, yoga, tai chi and qi gong and describes physiological transmutation as opposed to a mere psychological understanding. The ultimate achievement, the Rainbow Body, represents the complete physical transmutation of the human body into pure energy.

The full activation of the mind represents the future of brain science and will eventually result in a global Bodhisattva civilization. A Bodhisattva is an individual who seeks to enlighten all sentient beings so as to enable them to transcend all limitations and all suffering.

The Original Face is the starting point of the human body, which one sees when one's body is fully activated. It is this experience that enabled the Buddha to awaken completely under the Bodhi Tree. To see one's Original Face is the goal of real Zen and results in the realization of Tao. The original mind of each human being is ultimate freedom, the goal of life is to fully evolve and reunite the original mind with the mind of Tao, which represents complete inner illumination.

When it becomes understood that it is possible for each human being to permanently transcend birth and death as well as time and space, humanity will recognize its own true nature and become free.

Information on the film, called *The Lost Secret of Immortality*, based on this book, is available at www.lostsecretofimmortality.com.

Note: Many of the practices described in these pages are best learned from a teacher. You can find some excellent books and videos out there but, if at all possible, try to connect with a teacher. You will find that you will progress much faster and with fewer problems if you are working with a fully trained instructor. See the resources section at the end of this book for some websites that may be helpful.

The Embryo of Enlightenment
Sheng-t'ai and Tathagatagarbha

Syncretist movements combining Taoism, Buddhism, and Confucianism compare the Taoist *sheng-t'ai* to the Buddhist *tathagatagarbha* or the *dharmakaya*.

The term *sheng-t'ai* furthermore occurs in the writings of Tsung-mi, a patriarch of the Hua-yen School of Chinese Buddhism. In a passage on the origin of Zen, Tsung-mi speaks of nourishing the spirit (*shen*) and allowing the sacred embryo to grow. Ma-tzu Tao-i, one of the most famous Zen masters of the 8th century, also used the term.

The Shambhala Dictionary of Taoism

Comparing the development of the embryo to the revelation of Buddhahood is typical of *neidan* texts of the Ming period. For instance, the *Xingming guizhi* (Principles of Balanced Cultivation of Inner Nature and Vital Force) uses Body of the Law (*fashen, dharmakaya*) as a synonym for *shengtai*. The birth of the embryo represents the appearance of the original spirit (*yuanshen*) or Buddhahood and is understood as enlightenment. The process leading to the birth of the embryo consists of the purification of inner nature and vital force (*xing and ming*). Thus the true inner nature and vital force come into being, which in turn is equated to the return to emptiness. The embryo also indicates the unity of body (*shen*), heart (*xin*), and intention (*yi*) in a state of quiescence without motion.

Martina Darga, *Encyclopedia of Taoism*

CHAPTER ONE
Saintly Deaths and Disappearing Bodies

In 1998 a strange story emerged from a village in the remote Kham region of eastern Tibet. It is said that a rainbow appeared one day above the cabin of Khenpo A-Chos, a devout lama who had continued to practice and teach Buddhism despite the severe restrictions of the Chinese government. He was in his eighties, but not sick. Nevertheless, he lay down on his bed, began reciting the Tibetan mantra "Om mani padme hum," and died.

Shortly after the nuns, monks and others who studied with him began the Tibetan Buddhist prayers that accompany death, they noticed that Khenpo A-Chos' skin began to turn soft and pinkish. His students hurried to another lama to ask about this, and he told them to cover the body and continue their prayers. They placed a thin yellow monk's cloak over him and as the days passed they saw his body was shrinking. By the end of the week, the students reported, nothing remained – just a few hairs left on the pillow, Khenpo A-Chos had apparently become what is known in Tibetan Buddhism as a Rainbow Body.

The story spread through Buddhist circles, making its way to the United States, where Brother David Steindl-Rast, a Benedictine monk, heard it. He realized that the miraculous event had implications for Christianity: "If we can establish as an anthropological fact that what is described in the resurrection of Jesus had not only happened to others but is happening today," he said, "it would put our view of human potential in a completely different light."

Brother David enlisted the aid of Father Francis Tiso, an associate director of the secretariat for Ecumenical and Interreligious Affairs at the United States Conference of Catholic Bishops in Washington D.C., who also has a doctorate in Buddhist studies. Father Tiso journeyed to Kham with a translator and recorded the testimony of several people who had witnessed the events.

The lama who had been consulted by the students, Lama A-Chos (no relation) told him that achieving the rainbow body "is a matter of inner realization. It's not a philosophical idea. It's not a metaphor." He also showed Father Tiso photographs of himself, indicating what looked like light radiating from his body.

Jane Bosveld, Discover Magazine, June 07.

A body that shrinks away after death, the attainment of a Rainbow Body, is a rare phenomenon. It may, however, be the explanation for a multitude of ascension stories that have occurred throughout history and are described in cultures involving holy people at very high levels of spiritual development. Common to many civilizations are stories of holy men who exude light or become light at the end. Of course, we have many fully enlightened saints who left their bodies intact after death as well.

Here is another story of the Rainbow Body, found in Sushila Blackman's excellent book, *Graceful Exits: How Great Beings Die*, of the death of Sonam Namgyal, an itinerant stone carver of mantras and sacred texts. His family watched his body literally disappear after death.

Sonam was not thought of as an educated man, although it was said that he had received spiritual teachings from a great master in his youth. People often saw him sitting alone, gazing into space. He created mantras and wrote sacred songs, which he sang to himself. The surprising tale of his life and death started in 1952 when he became ill, yet at the same time, increasingly happy. Doctors were called, who apparently could do nothing to cure him of his grave illness. Sonam grew increasingly weak, yet appeared almost joyful to those who visited him.

At one point, his son encouraged him to remember the spiritual teachings given to him in his youth by the great master, but Sonam smiled gently and said quietly, "I've forgotten them all and anyway, there's nothing to remember. Everything is an illusion. But I am confident that all is well."

Upon his deathbed, he asked only for one thing. He asked that no one should move his body for one week. So after he died, his family wrapped his body in clean clothes and placed him in a small room that seemed to mysteriously accommodate his large body. They invited monks and lamas to sit with the body, to complete the practices common to their beliefs and culture, to correctly honor his death and assist his passing, as was their custom. Everyone noticed one thing that was quite odd; the house seemed to have a significant aura within it. A rainbow-colored light danced on the walls. Then on the sixth day after Sonam's death, they were surprised to see that his body had significantly changed. It was obviously smaller than it had been in the days before. Every time they looked in, they saw that his body had become even smaller. On the eighth day after his death, the morning scheduled for the funeral, undertakers came to remove his body. They carefully unwrapped the

5

cloth covering his corpse, finding much to their surprise, nothing left inside but fingernails and wisps of hair. [1]

Like Sonam's apparently happy death, there are many stories in both Buddhism and Taoism of masters who seemed to know about and welcome their oncoming death. They prepared for their passing with courage, equanimity and grace. One such story comes from ancient China.

Wang Zhe, the founder of Quanzhen Taoism – one of the two most ancient Taoist sects, died in 1170. Just prior to his death he proclaimed to all of his students that he was about to "return" to the Tao. His students begged him to leave some final instruction for them. He replied that he already had and showed them the following verse:

Master Chonyang of Difei (the Zhongnan mountains),
[People] call [him] Lunatic Wang.
When he comes [into the world] to nurture the sun and moon.
After he leaves [the world] he will entrust himself to the west and
     east [roam freely].
He makes himself a companion of the clouds and streams.
He makes himself a neighbor with the empty void.
His singly numinous Real Nature exists.
It is not the same with the minds of the masses.

Then, after warning his disciples not to weep or mourn for him, Wang Zhe lay down on his side using his bent left elbow as a pillow, and he passed away.

Stephen Eskildsen, *The Teaching and Practices of the Early Quanzhen Taoist Masters*. [2]

Another story of a saintly death, also included in Sushila Blackman's book, tells of Zen Master Kanzan Egen. He began teaching in the Buddhist tradition late in life, at 60 years of age. A severe taskmaster, he trained a small, select group of students. He was parsimonious in his selection of koans, or teaching statements. Of the few he used, his favorite was, "For Egen, here there is no birth and death".

One day, he contacted his sole heir and charged him with the

1 *Graceful Exits: How Great Beings Die* by Sushila Blackman, Shambala Publications, 2005.

2 *The Teaching and Practices of the Early Quanzhen Taoist Masters*, Stephen Eskildsen, State University of New York Press, 2004.

6

responsibility of his affairs. He dressed in clothes he normally wore when planning to travel and quietly left. He went and stood by himself at the Temple's front gate, beside the wind and water pond. And there he died.

We know from biblical accounts that Jesus of Nazareth also knew of his coming death. Prior to his famous last supper, Jesus Christ revealed his body of light. He took Peter, James, and John to the top of a mountain. To their utter amazement his face began to shine with a heavenly light and his clothing became a dazzling and unearthly white. The long dead saints, Moses and Elijah, appeared from out of nowhere. Jesus instructed his disciples to speak to no one about any of this until after he himself had risen from the dead. The disciples did not understand what he meant, this rising from the dead, until later.

After he suffered torture and an excruciatingly painful death, soldiers poked with their spears at Jesus' dead body, still hanging on the cross at his crucifixion. Only then would they allow his body to be taken away for burial. Joseph of Arimathea, an honored member of the Jewish Supreme Court and a secret disciple of Jesus, had gathered his courage and boldly went to Pontius Pilate who gave him permission to take away the body of Jesus. So Joseph was allowed to take the lifeless body away, while Roman guards closely watched. Then he and Nicodemus, who brought a hundred pounds of embalming ointment made of myrrh and aloes, tended to Jesus' body. Together they wrapped his body in a long linen cloth saturated with the spices and put him in a new tomb in a grove of trees.

Early Sunday morning, Mary Magdelene went to the tomb and found the rock covering the entrance had been rolled away. She ran and got Simon Peter and John to help, thinking someone had stolen Jesus' body. John arrived first and saw the body was indeed gone. All he saw was the long cloth wrap on the floor. Simon Peter arrived on his footsteps and also saw the empty shroud as well as the swath that had covered his head lying in a bundle on the side.

His earthly body was never seen again but Jesus appeared to his disciples in a new body several times before he ascended to Heaven. According to John, many miracles were performed but the most important thing was to let people know that believing in him as the Son of God would give them life, immortality.

Whether Christian, Buddhist, Taoist, Hindu, or Shamanic, many spiritual paths have stories of ascension and share a common belief in humankind's ability to gain immortality. These stories were simply told here as examples of what can be achieved by fully enlightened people.

These masters faced their own deaths with grace and non-attachment. Some even caused their bodies to shrink and emit light. One can say that they were able to reach enlightenment or become as "one with the Tao" or that they had attained nirvana, snuffing out all attachments to the material world.

While these stories of ancient masters seem like unattainable heights of consciousness and transcendence of the physical, the most incredible fact is that this ability is available to every man and woman.

Yes, that same ability is within you. At this very moment, you have begun to unravel the mysteries, the secrets of immortality that lie waiting for you to discover.

This book reveals the secrets of the cosmos contained within your body. Our lives are completely within our control. We all have special powers.

We can unlock the keys to health, happiness, peace, joy and wealth by working with the energies that we were all born with.

Humankind has known this truth for thousands of years. Attempts to express and activate these secrets are documented and recorded. Now, thanks to better translations of ancient texts and improved teaching and access to information, all humans have the opportunity to use their true selves to transform their lives, and transform this world.

This transfiguration can happen, body by body, by body. And you have it within you already.

At the beginning of this chapter, you read about the curious disappearance of Khenpo A-Cho's body. The Rainbow Body, that ultimate transition of body into spirit of Buddhist lore, is something that has been documented for centuries in Tibetan history. It has been linked to a system of inner alchemy called Ati Yoga. Experiencing ultimate enlightenment, called Seeing the Original Face by Buddhists or the Golden Embryo by Taoists, is mentioned again and again in the mystical texts of India, Japan and China. All these religious philosophies –whether Tibetan Buddhism, Hinduism, Zen, Taoism (Daoism), Christianity, or Shamanism–have the common denominator of the "perennial philosophy", the core of individual and collective mystical experience. This is a view that sees the world as divided into two aspects: the invisible, unified, unmanifest, implicit, mystical level of reality and the visible, manifold, manifest, explicit, material level of reality (the latter is understood as derived from and secondary to the former). This is considered the universal philosophy. The inner alchemical experience then is to unite the two aspects, to attain enlightenment, and to gain those special powers available to the fully enlightened human. Successful spiritual alchemy is available to all of us; everyone is capable.

A Rainbow Body is a body not made of flesh, but consisting of pure light. Advanced methods enable one to reach Total Realization...at which point the physical body dissolves into the essence of its elements, which is light.

A Rainbow Body

Thangka image from www.thangkapaintings.com

A good place to begin is to look at the physical body and its relationship to consciousness. All you need is your body and your mind to begin the journey to complete enlightenment and experience the superpowers of the masters.

Ancient secrets are being unlocked.

Herein, those locks and keys will be examined. You, like countless others, will be shown the way down the path. Guidelines and exercises will describe the way to reach those truths. They are accessible to all humankind because the mysterious source of energy is found within every human body, the original energy. The culmination of following these guidelines and exercises may result in the Rainbow Body. Whether that will be your experience is uncertain, but what is certain is that you can expect an increase in health, happiness and longevity.

The keys to the profound treasures in your mind and your body are available now. The secrets of immortality shall be revealed. The power is within!

The way to begin is with your body and your mind.

KEY CONCEPTS
- The Rainbow Body represents the complete physical transmutation of the human body into pure energy.
- One's own body can be used as the first step toward psychological and spiritual wholeness.
- Ancient physical systems were developed to unlock the mysterious source of our energy.
- By practicing these systems, you can activate spiritual wholeness, as well as increase health, prosperity and longevity, and attain ultimate spiritual freedom, or enlightenment.

CHAPTER TWO
Beginning with the Body

Man is the measure of all things.
    Pythagoras

Within your body exists all the answers to all questions ever asked.

Throughout history, humankind has sought healing for the wounds or illnesses of the body as well as answers to fundamental questions that trouble a serious thinking mind. Some particularly lucky or gifted people have sought and found high levels of fulfillment. And some of these lucky few created disciplines and traditions, often hidden from repressive societies, so that others might follow their footsteps to better health, expansion of mind, and freedom of soul and spirit.

Today, greater freedom of press and speech has liberated information from within these disciplines. Anyone has access to what mystics, seers, philosophers, thinkers and spiritual pilgrims sought throughout the ages. Access to this information is not just possible, it is easy. The challenge is to fully comprehend these truths. Attempts to explain them have sometimes been misunderstood. It is time now to clarify and explain all the secrets.

You don't have to visit a temple in Japan and sit with Buddhist monks in a peaceful monastery wisped with jasmine incense. You don't have to bathe in the River Ganges with Hindus, as the bright morning sun glimmers on the holy water, or sip a cup of hot soothing butter tea with the Dalai Lama as you gaze upon the majestic Himalayas. You don't have to lie on a leather couch receiving psychological analysis from a spectacled man with a goatee. You most certainly don't have to clatter about in a laboratory with alchemists, trying to turn lead into gold.

Many have used just such paths in their soul search for answers to the human questions, "Who am I? How did I get here? How can I be happy and fulfilled? What is my destiny?" Now the possibility of gaining the answers to these questions, and more, are available to you through disciplines developed through the ages, happily communicated to you through teachers. You can practice them in your living room, during your coffee break at work, or in a clearing by a pristine brook bubbling through a springtime wood. Location and schedule is your choice.

11

The answers to your deepest questions are closer than you think. Because, wherever you are, you will find the answers to all questions. The truth you seek is within you, in what Jesus Christ described as the "Temple of the Holy Spirit." The truth is within your body. Your body is the doorway to truth.

And what an amazing doorway it is for such a task! The human body is an incredible creation with amazing potential that has worked beautifully and efficiently for many centuries. Within it are systems of circulation, muscles, nerves, and reproduction; all of which have worked the same since the beginning of human existence. Listen to evolutionary biologists and you'll know that humans, and the human body as it is today, have been around for tens of thousands of years. Even if you abide by creationist theories, the human body has been the same for at least six thousand years.

The blood that Jesus bled had corpuscles and hemoglobin. The saints and every man, woman, and child have this in common – a working corporeal body that functions in similar ways in order to support life. We all have hearts that pump blood and lungs that bring in oxygen. Without a working heart and lungs our brains would be deprived of oxygen and our bodies would cease to function. We would die. We all reside in our bodies.

To say that all humans have bodies would be over-simplistic. After all, all creatures, great and small, have bodies, from thundering elephants to amoeba squiggling along in pools of water. It is also true that humans have different kinds of bodies. We come in all sizes and shapes – tall, short, thin, round, male, female. Of course, male and female bodies have unique properties that identify them as different. The properties of the two sexes are echoed in nature, according to traditional Chinese philosophy, as yin/yang.

Michelangelo and his Renaissance peers like Leonardo da Vinci glorified the human body in their art and science. Michelangelo's realistic statue of David celebrates the beauty of the human body – the definition of muscles, the strength and shape of his limbs. Leonardo's famous drawing, Anatomy of Man, was even used as a teaching tool for doctors to understand the layout of muscles and bone structure. The proportions of the human body in his drawing demonstrated a combination of scientific and artistic understanding. That was Leonardo's intent – to combine art with science, man with nature.

Yes, the human body is remarkable on its own, but Leonardo, like many others, saw that it was more than just a physiological system. To be human is more than just to exist within a body.

There is an energy within our bodies. It moves us to interact and enhances our sensory perceptions. When peace conferences occur, what do the representatives of opposing factions do, besides hopefully settle their differences? They eat and drink together, a moment of intimacy and fulfillment of a common human need. Sharing a meal lets down the barriers between people. Together, we share pleasure in the taste and texture and color of foods. We taste salty, bitter, sour, sweet, and the earthy flavors of umami in our meals. We crunch on raw slices of cucumber, round red radishes, and sticks of carrot root. We admire the color combinations of an artfully prepared salad; a green base of lettuce with bright slices of red tomato, topped with purple rings of onion and orange nests of shredded carrot. We smell popcorn in a dark theater. On a morning walk, we notice our neighbors who are cooking breakfast, the smells of bacon frying and coffee brewing.

And together we also share emotional moments. People laugh in concert at comedy performances and cry together at funerals. We celebrate attainment of goals and landmark moments, in another person's life or our own. So families gather for graduation ceremonies and weddings. Emotional energy pulls us together and spurs us to strive toward our highest goals.

Opportunities to interact bring people closer. We sit in crowded theaters to see movies on the big screen or live performances of plays. We partner up to hit a tennis ball across a net and watch to see it returned, so we can smack it back. Together we dance to the rhythm of our culture's music. Attraction energizes us and gives us greater quality of life.

Shared ideas and beliefs bring us into more contact. We go to school to learn together so that we can experience the joy of interactive learning. We sit in coffee shops in small groups, sipping coffee or tea, and discuss and debate the day's news.

We also interact within our bodies. Our bodies can be great sources of pain and pleasure. Cuts and burns and bruises hurt. Hugs and caresses and sexual union bring us joy.

So we begin with the body. The original energy of the body is the starting point, the source. If that original energy is heated through a variety of techniques, such as breathing practices, meditation, visualization, mantras, and potentially even sexual yoga, the energy meridians of the

13

body open and the original energy of the body supercharges the brain.

When we integrate all levels of body, mind, and spirit, that energy which flows through the body combines with the energy of spirit, the energy of the universe. The techniques described herein are all meant to assist you in fully opening the energy meridians of the body. Then the mind, the body, and the energy systems become unified and then you can achieve your full potential, which is realization, enlightenment or superconsciousness.

Super powers become accessible. Health, happiness and longevity increase.

KEY CONCEPTS
- The human body has not altered significantly since the first man.
- The body has many functions and is made up of different systems.
- The body includes an energy system.
- When looking at the concept of body-mind-spirit, we look first at the body.
- The starting point of enlightenment is in the body.
- Techniques can heat the original energy for increased flow through the meridians, to supercharge the brain.
- A result is increased health, happiness, and longevity.

CHAPTER THREE
The Human Mind – Science or Illusion

Just as all humans have bodies, we can generally agree that our bodies have minds, though sometimes we lose them!

Although humans are not the largest of this planet's creatures, we are the most complex. We have nervous systems and brains that, over the course of maturation, develop what we call the mind. A mind is a product of genetics, conditioning, purposeful learning, and experiences. It functions as a receptacle for memories, creates our personal identities, and shapes the traits that we call our unique personality. Our mind contains all of our thoughts and emotions.

It is a combination of physical and energetic processes. Neurotransmitters fire up when we are in love or deeply afraid. Science has proven there are different functions for different parts of the brain. Areas of Wiernecke and Broca contain language centers for verbal processing. The amydgala and hippocampus protect and keep our memories of facts and emotional connections. Brain scans have shown that there is an infinite variety of patterns of activity in each area. Some areas may be overactive or low in activity and these differences correspond with different ways that people think or feel.

Because the brain is always active, thoughts and ideas continuously process what our bodies sense, what our experiences have taught, and what our minds perceive as possibilities for the future. A mind has hopes and fears. Some are based on logic and experience; some are simply illusions derived from the infinite possibilities open to us or what we have been taught. Some things we know from facts; some things we know from faith. Some things are dreamt.

Every mind is thus unique. Some minds – through works of art, philosophy, science, or lessons given – have left us a legacy of knowledge and beliefs. We talk about the great minds of history like Lao Tzu (Laozi), Confucius, The Buddha, Jesus Christ, Socrates, Aristotle, Plato, Milarepa, Galileo, Leonardo da Vinci, William Shakespeare, Descartes, Newton, Charles Darwin and Albert Einstein.

Even with their abilities, it might be argued that these were simply bodies with brains that worked better than most, and some scientists have argued just that. Pull the plug on the body, blink! Off goes the mind. Or so it seems.

However, even before modern science began its work, humans noticed that they seemed to own some other quality. Working with minds and bodies, they searched for that quality, and they explored the universe beyond their touch and sight, their taste and hearing.

The ancient Egyptians looked up to the sun arcing over the sky by day, just as the Mayans looked up at the glittering stars, and they wondered what was the meaning behind their lives, their minds, and their bodies.

Then again, many of the Eastern philosophies call what we experience as "the real world" a construct of the mind. We have a perceived reality, created by our experience, wisdom, conditioning, and beliefs. This mind, with its many layers, like that of an onion, fools us into thinking that this world, this experience, is "real" and the world of spirit is somehow not as real. This, say the Eastern mystics, is actually the opposite of what is true, that our experiences are illusions and that the spirit is all that is truly real.

The Greek philosopher Plato also taught about the illusions created by the mind in his allegory of prisoners in a cave.

He instructed his students to imagine a group of prisoners chained in a wide area of a deep cave so that they can only face a wall. Behind them is a fire. Between the fire and the prisoners is a conveyor belt, carrying plants, animals and objects. The only reality the prisoners know is the flickering shadows they see cast on the wall of themselves and the contents of the conveyor belt. They do not comprehend that they are prisoners.

Suppose one of these prisoners notices his chains. Suppose he figures out how to free himself. He turns and sees what's really going on. Moreover, he notices light coming down a tunnel. He climbs up through the tunnel and emerges into our world and sees the true sun.

Should he continue further in this new adventure?

No, suggests Plato. He should return to the cave, convince his fellow prisoners of this greater reality and help liberate them from their shackles in the darkness of the cave.

The illusion of a false reality limits human potential. To be free of the illusion allows us to go back to the genius lying dormant within. Our secret identity within has limitless powers. Activating our original energy enables us to reach our full potential.

Original energy represents this ultimate potential, our secret identity, the superhero that resides in all of us. Freedom from the shackles of illusion reveals our secret identities, our true selves.

The illusion is the trap of believing that what is outside ourselves is real and that what is inside doesn't matter. Spiritual freedom is knowing that what is real is what is inside. Our existence is enriched; our ultimate potential is tapped. Our powers are increased and we can realize our full potential with the techniques that are no longer held secret from us. We can achieve superconsciousness, immortality or Buddhahood. It is available to all of us now.

In the present existence, mired in the illusion of our lives and the mechanical nature of culture and society, we are held prisoners. Using the ideas in this book, we can free ourselves from the shackles of the cave and find true reality.

Then, in the tradition of the Bodhisattvas, as spiritual teachers, we can turn around and liberate our fellow prisoners.

It is Reality that we actually experience every day, all of us, but reality that we've ignored because we have not been taught how to see it. It is an omission of our culture and society as we are conditioned by the imputed societal beliefs of how it should be.

But, you ask, how can reality change?

Reality can change because we can change.

The whole point of moving onward in understanding is loosening rigid and frozen assumptions, of letting go of attachments to conceptual thinking that mask the hidden truths within us.

How then does this mind create such a beguiling and seemingly concrete world? And how can we use this same mind to free ourselves from this illusion and dwell in the infinite?

These are questions that have baffled many philosophers and spiritual seekers over the centuries. And yet, as we shall see, there is a body of knowledge and experience that we can draw upon to attain just this freedom.

KEY CONCEPTS
- Nervous systems and the brain form and support the mind.
- The mind is a combination of physiology, energy and consciousness.
- The mind functions as a receptacle of thought, emotion and belief.

- What the mind perceives as real is a result of conditioning and teaching.
- Thoughts are based on facts, beliefs and illusion.
- Removing the illusion brings spiritual freedom, revealing the full potential that lies within us.
- Original energy represents the ultimate potential, the superhero within.

CHAPTER FOUR
Splitting Spirit and Science

It seems like common sense. We know we have a body, and we know we have a mind. But it often feels like there's something more to life. It feels like there's some almost intangible instinct within our mind and body that wants to lead us beyond the physical into the world of spirit. Some call that a soul, but we shall call it spirit, a word derived from the Latin word for breath. Just as a body is informed with breath, so body and mind are informed with spirit.

So, it follows that if the body seems to produce our minds, and our body is the creation of the reproduction of our mother's and father's bodies, then our spirits are the product of something beyond that.

We're not only told we have spirit by spiritual teachers, but it just seems right. It certainly helps make sense of things. Our bodies die, and sometimes our minds go before our bodies. Who are we really? Do we exist for nothing? Is there something that remains of us after death beyond a corpse or ashes?

Religion and spiritual teachings comfort us and provide meaning to our lives. A comforted and meaning-filled spirit and mind certainly feels right in human bodies.

Yet minds wonder about the meaning of other things. For instance, minds wondered about the sun. For some races of early humans the sun was God, or at least, like Apollo in Greek myth, a god. We would not exist without the sun. The sun is our main source of energy. However we would not exist if our planet was closer to the sun, or further away. It is a perfect balance.

Early humans, in their simple observational scientific mode, just looked up and saw the sun's progress across the sky. Since things seemed to pretty much stay still, it was easy to assume that the sun, and the stars, moon and planets traveled around us. Earth, after all, was the center of the cosmos. That was the reality for their times.

By the late Middle Ages and a bit beyond, the Roman Catholic Church pretty much had a grip on political matters in Europe and dictated all beliefs and truths. Reality was defined by those beliefs and truths.

The trouble with the spirit is that since it's so hard to qualify or quantify for an individual, most people look to a higher authority to interpret and explain what we need to know about spirit. So in those times, the higher authority was Papal Rome and their explanations were not to be questioned. The Church was so adamant in their view of reality that they became social and cultural bullies to anyone who defied or questioned their views.

So while the Roman Catholic Church was quite happy with the work Michelangelo did painting the ceiling of the Sistine Chapel, they were not so happy about what else was developing. With greater access to education and ancient texts, like the works of the Greek philosopher Aristotle, inquiring human beings started becoming bravely curious and questioning the status quo.

Perhaps the earth wasn't flat!

Astronomers like Copernicus began to suggest in fact that the sun didn't orbit the Earth. Quite the opposite! The Earth orbited the Sun, which was just one star amongst a myriad of suns. Heresy!

Worse, the astronomer Galileo began to prove this, using a system that apparently frightened the dictators of spiritual affairs of the era so much that they wanted to kill him. Science and Church ran smack into each other and so began the great illusion, that science and spirit were separate; that there was no integrating the two.

This was the beginning of modern science wherein the scientific method as proof was demanded to override long held beliefs. The scientific method involves using carefully designed research techniques for investigating every material thing in our world, thus acquiring new knowledge, as well as for correcting and integrating previous knowledge. It is based on gathering observable, empirical, measurable evidence, and tested by creating experiments that take into account a variety of possible variables. Results are usually recreated and repeated so that there is little room for doubt of the findings. The new information was tested and proven beyond a doubt, but you couldn't argue with the Church's official beliefs.

Galileo's scientific work upset the Catholic Church so much that they accused him of heresy. That was a very serious charge, because, in those days, heretics were publicly burned to death.

The Catholic Church had a history of giving short shrift to heretics. In the year 1209, the town of Beziers in the Languedoc region in southern France near the Mediterranean Sea, was attacked by legions of the Church because its inhabitants would not recant their religious doctrines of Catharism, a form of Christian Gnosticism becoming popular at the time. The Cathars held a dualistic belief that material things and the pursuit of power were separate from the higher principles of love and that both could not exist together. This was a direct assault against the power of the Catholic Church and its richness of land, jewels, gold, and art. So a crusade against the Cathars was ordered by Rome and knights from Northern France were sent to the area. Given that some of the town's populace were good Catholics, one of the Catholic army officers asked Arnaud, the Abbott-commander, how soldiers of the Pope-approved God could tell Cathar from Catholic.

"Caedite eos. Novit enim Dominus qui sunt eius," replied Arnaud. "Kill them all. The Lord will recognize His own."

As many as 20,000 men, women and children were slaughtered.

And in 1633, in the midst of the Spanish Inquisition, the Church still could be ruthless in these spiritual matters, so it was prudent on Galileo's part to recant his ideas on the position of the Earth in the universe.

Still, the cat was out of the bag. Science continued, and scientists continued to search for truth through the scientific method, though often in secret to avoid the scrutiny of church leaders. Science and Spirit were divided, on opposing sides from that point in time, with little attempt to bring them back together. Religion became the antithesis to truth for the world of science, a fund of legend and myth.

Until the twentieth century, with the rise of technology and communication between cultures, all that began to change. In our more global community of the twenty-first century, the doors have been more widely opened to the beliefs and truths of Eastern medicine and philosophy. The Eastern cultures did not experience the same split of spirit and science. Even within the repressive policies of Communist regimes, the Eastern medical practices continued to use spiritual energy to heal and promote health.

Now we hear more and more reports of scientific research attempting to bring the duality of science and spirit back together. There have been more than 600 scientific studies, for instance, relating the benefits of meditation on health and well-being, according to the official website for Transcendental Meditation.

What can scientists make of soul and spirit? A famous study was done by Dr. Duncan MacDougall in 1907. He was present at the deaths of six people, who were cared for at the end while lying on a special bed resting on a platform of beam scales in his office. At the moment of their death, he found a sudden drop in weight of approximately ¾ of an ounce, or 21 grams, which he attributed to the weight of the human soul. His interest in empirical proof for the human soul continued with attempts to photograph the soul in x-rays, which doesn't appear to have succeeded prior to his own death.

But MacDougall was unusual for having tried to connect science and spirit. It was more often that scientists worked to disprove the existence of spirit. Much has been documented regarding scientific experts discovering fraudulent practices of spiritualists in the midst of séances. For the most part, it has been much more popular in the scientific community to scoff at spirit as myth rather than as truth.

Still, even today, scientists who are not agnostics or atheists tend to compartmentalize their faiths.

So in Western religion and science, the concept of fusing body, mind, and spirit is relatively recent. But in Eastern religions and medicine, the split between religion and science did not happen. As we become aware of, learn about, and adopt Eastern medical practices such as yoga, qi gong and meditation, we accept the concepts of the holistic viewpoint. Body, mind, and spirit are intertwined and inseparable once you look at the whole picture. The fact is that acupuncture, once only practiced in Asia, is now accepted in the United States as an insurance-approved medical treatment that works by unblocking the energy meridians in the body.

In this body-mind-spirit paradigm, there is a corporeal physical level, a mental level of thought, and an energetic level. When these levels are integrated and united by fully opening the energy meridians of the body, then the mind, body and energy systems become unified. When the energy meridians in the body are fully opened through these practices, the energy of the body and the energy of the universe are united.

What is this mysterious source of energy? In the East, they call the body's vitality qi (chi), so spirit is qi. And when qi is fully refined, it appears as the Golden Spirit or Original Spirit. Qi is present in everyone and it is the original energy that is present in you before birth. In fact, in your life, between conception and birth, your original energy was enlightened. Your spirit was in its purest form in this pre-birth body. All your meridians were wide open while you lived as an embryo within your mother's body. After birth, your breathing pattern changed from your lower abdomen to your upper chest. As your breathing changed, there was a disconnect from the original source. The change in breathing started the aging process, resulting in weaker qi and partially blocked meridians.

But rest assured. The techniques you can use in tai chi (tai ji), qi gong (chi gong), and other breathing practices can retrain your breathing pattern. Your breath can revert back to the baby's pattern of breathing, creating greater and stronger qi. The aging process can be reversed. You may recreate conception within your body by using techniques that create enough heat to fully activate the starting point of the body. And then you return to the embryonic stage of enlightenment, which is the goal.

Why? Because, for your mind, the ultimate in mental freedom is enlightenment. For your body, the greater the flow of qi, the healthier and stronger you will be. And because qi is spirit, bringing it back to the source of the original energy is enlightenment at the highest level.

According to ancient Chinese medical theory, the starting point in the human body is the Spiritual Embryo. It is the secret of enlightenment or immortality, the embryo of Buddhahood. It is whole and it lies dormant in all humans. When it is fully activated, it is said to appear as a golden embryonic version of the meditator at the culmination of enlightenment.

In India, the religion of Buddhism not only considered the issues of body, mind and spirit —it had created a word to speak of their unity.

The word is trikaya.

KEY CONCEPTS
- Spirit gives meaning to lives and defines who we are beyond body and mind.
- Spirit is difficult to quantify or qualify and as such has traditionally been the province of religious authority.
- Scientific experiments that discovered facts contrary to the official viewpoint of the Roman Catholic Church were considered to be heresy, a death sentence for scientists who wouldn't conform to church teachings.
- A split occurred between science and religion in the Western world.
- Science and spirituality are beginning to reunite as scientists study effects of Eastern medical and meditation practices.
- In Eastern thought, spirit is "qi," which is the original energy

that is found in everyone.

- Original qi is enlightened in the embryonic stage between conception and birth.
- Mind, body, and spirit are fully united when meridians are opened.
- A fully activated mind is the ultimate in mental freedom.
- Strong qi makes healthy bodies.
- Enlightenment is the embryonic level of qi and may be seen as an image of the Golden Embryo of our own prebirth existence.

CHAPTER FIVE
Three Bodies:
The Trikaya of Buddhism

The religion of the future will be a cosmic religion. The religion which is based on experience, which refuses the dogmatic. If there is any religion that would cope with scientific needs, that would be Buddhism.
Albert Einstein

Why did the esteemed scientist, Albert Einstein, endorse Buddhism? Because Buddhism, in its efforts to gather information and qualify and quantify elements of body, mind, and spirit, looks to be a model for Western science as it gazes into the deep structure of consciousness and examines such practices as meditation. As Western science tackles the questions of spiritual illumination, Tantric Buddhism provides a possible framework from which to begin multiple lines of research.

Buddhism has always maintained a unity of thinking about body-soul-spirit. Originally Western culture had the same thought. The Latin concept of corpus-anima-spiritus refers to the combination of body-soul-spirit. But when European scientists split from the Church, going underground to secretly continue controversial scientific research, the two factions of science and religion divided into separate schools of thought. Meanwhile, in China, Tibet and India, medicine, science and spirituality were not separated. Their systems are intact to this day.

And East and West are no longer split in thought due to the increasingly global community.

Rudyard Kipling said "East is East and West is West and never the twain shall meet."

Kipling was of course, talking about culture and society. He has been proved dead wrong by a twenty-first century where East and West are meeting constantly. Buddhism is no longer unheard of in Western culture. More and more, people have become familiar with the previously mysterious philosophy, beliefs, and customs of Eastern medicine and religion. Millions of people throughout the world are now doing yoga. Acupuncture is covered by insurance. Westerners have embraced the Eastern practices of meditation and tai chi.

The Tantric Buddhists, who started these spiritual disciplines, had no special powers built into their physiology. They had precisely the same abilities as we do now, yet they used them differently to an effect that can be recreated by anyone, given the correct techniques. You have the potential to attain the same level of true Buddhahood. You have the same power.

Their goal was enlightenment, and it can be yours, by fully integrating and uniting the energy of spirit, body, and mind. They called this unity trikaya, a Sanskrit word. Although we use it here to imply unity of body, mind and spirit, in fact it literally means three bodies – though very different bodies indeed.

The first of the three bodies in Buddhism (Northern Buddhism to be precise) is nirmanakaya, which represents the physical body of a Buddha. The sambhogakaya represents the dream or bliss body of a Buddha. This corresponds with the Chinese yin subtle body. The dharmakaya represents the reality or truth body, which is holographic, superconscious and outside of space and time. In China, this would be the yang subtle body, which is totally dormant until it awakens in enlightenment. It is also known as the Embryo of Buddahood, created at the point of conception (bindu) within the human body – The Original Face.

We've also heard the Latin version, the corpus or physical body, the anima or soul, and spiritus or spirit. That is the trinity, the alchemical union that many civilizations described as the ultimate goal of fusing the two inner subtle bodies within the physical body. In Western alchemy this was known as the Philosopher's Stone.

These exotic sounding names more or less correspond with body, soul, and spirit. The Chinese concept of the unity of the physical body, the yin subtle body, and the yang subtle body is thus the same as our Western body-soul-spirit trio. By unifying these three bodies, it was said that any individual could transcend birth, death, space and time. Once the trikaya was attained, enlightenment and omniscience followed.

Combining separate bodies into one body is and was a highly prized accomplishment in many cultures. The conjunction of opposites was mentioned in the majority of alchemical texts. If you look within Islamic texts of 500 years ago, Greco-Egyptian texts of 1000 years ago, and ancient Chinese texts – all have different terminology describing this union. Whether it is heaven and earth, sun and moon, yin and yang, male and female, fire and water; all describe the union of two subtle bodies because that represents ultimate spiritual awakening and immortality, the ancient quest for perfect self-realization.

The trikaya is the triple point of consciousness in the same way that in physics, the triple point of water – a single combination of pressure and temperature at which point ice, water, and mist can coexist – are in equilibrium for all of its three states: solid, liquid and vapor. Interestingly, this harmony of the three states of water is also a Chinese metaphor for the union of body, soul, and spirit.

We find the concept of the trikaya mirrored and echoed in Eastern and Western philosophy, religion and science constantly, all the way from the Christian concept of God in three persons – the Holy Trinity of Father, Son, and Holy Spirit – to the Chinese concept of Heaven, Earth and Humanity.

Carl Jung, the Swiss psychiatrist, best known for his theories of the Collective Unconscious, including the concept of archetypes, and the use of synchronicity in psychotherapy, gave this conjunction a psychological interpretation, "the union of the unconscious reconciling with the conscious mind."

Three seems to be the number for perfect balance. Climbers learn about the safety of keeping three limbs securely fixed, while only moving the fourth. Somehow humans have always noticed they needed a combination of things to get life right, to be well-balanced. You can't work all the time. You can't play all the time. And much as some would like to, you can't sleep all the time. Yet it seems we need all three to keep things going right. All in balance.

Although not always with the same results. You will find different versions of the unification of the trikaya. At one extreme, the most complete version of this unification results in the dissolution of the physical body after death. This is called the Rainbow Body, "nirvana without remainder" or "assumption." Individuals who attain this peak, like those in the opening stories, leave corpses that actually shrink away within a week or two after death, disappearing completely. Or more radically, the body dissolves immediately after death, sometimes leaving nothing, sometimes leaving hair and fingernails. This trikaya, or union, may well have been an actual physical achievement for Lao Tzu, Jesus Christ and the Buddha, who represent enlightenment in their respective civilizations.

To follow the story of Buddha, we must travel from palace to Bodhi tree for his awakening. Shakyamuni Buddha, our historical source of Buddhism, lived from 563 to 483 BC. He was born as Prince Siddhartha and grew up living in great luxury and comfort. Just after the prince

27

was born, his father consulted a holy man about the future of his young son. The holy man told the king that Prince Siddhartha was destined for success as either a great spiritual leader or a powerful king. His father preferred that his son be a great king and carry on in his place. So he made plans to keep Siddhartha captive in the palace, far from any temptation or contact with holy men. Thereafter, the young prince spent his days in luxury, never being in the presence of anything or anyone that would distract him from his role as heir apparent. The king even made a decree that no one who was sick or old could be seen in the prince's presence. So naturally, Siddhartha grew up thinking that everyone was strong, young and healthy.

Eventually Prince Siddhartha married a lovely woman and they had a child. Now he had everything that he could imagine needing or wanting. However, he had never in his life left the royal compound. And he was curious about that. He wondered if there was anything new to see beyond the palace walls.

One day, after much effort, he talked his best friend, Channa, into smuggling him out of the palace so that he could see the rest of the city. It was only meant as a lark, but Siddhartha was shocked to see beggars in the streets. He saw emaciated children, their thin bones a stark contrast to the well fed visitors, staff, and royal family members he knew within the palace walls. He thought of his own child's chubby little arms, hair that shown and face that glowed with good health and showed dimples when he smiled. He saw nothing like that in these children, with their sad, thin, dirty little faces and dull, limp hair. He saw old people, bent over from pain and poor diet, shuffling along with their cups for alms. He saw blind people and people with unhealed sores and all kinds of deformities that he had never even imagined, some just sitting along the road with begging bowls.

Much disturbed in his heart and mind and soul, he asked his friend, "What is wrong with these people?"

"These people are sick or injured," answered Channa.

Then Prince Siddhartha pointed to an old man hobbling along painfully, with his head sunken down into his shoulders.

"What is wrong with that man," he asked, "is he sick also?"

"No, my prince," answered Channa. "He is merely old. We are all subject to aging, if we don't die young from sickness or injury."

Siddhartha was shocked. "How can it be," he cried, "that I have never seen this?"

Channa was wary of offending the king but he was Siddhartha's greatest friend and so told him the truth, how his father had intentionally kept all of this from him for all of his life.

The sight of all this misery overwhelmed Prince Siddhartha. Now he had witnessed suffering and he was appalled and sad. He had no idea that such misery existed. He couldn't continue on as he had before. He couldn't put the pictures out of his mind. Siddhartha felt compelled to act.

It is said that Siddhartha was so upset by what he had seen that he decided to leave the palace and go out into the world where he could seek the answers to all the many questions that now crowded into his head. So that night, after kissing his sleeping wife and child, he crept from the palace, where Channa was waiting for him just outside the walls.

Siddhartha went forth into the world alone with nothing but the beautiful robe that he wore in the palace, although that fine garment would soon become rags. He found other seekers and talked to them. He consulted with holy men. What he soon realized was that, to find the answers to his many questions, he needed to embark on a spiritual quest. So he entered the jungle where wild sadhus lived. He lived with these seekers of spiritual truths for years, performing many acts of asceticism until he almost died from malnutrition.

Even then he hadn't found the answers he sought. So after he recovered and gained back his health, he decided that the answer did not lie in punishing his body and practicing austerities. He realized that there must be a "middle way," something between severe asceticism and worldly entanglements. He left the jungle where he had lived with the sadhus, and traveled until he came to the present city of Bodhgaya in India. He decided to go no further. So there he sat under a Bodhi tree to meditate, first making a vow to sit in meditation until he realized his true self.

And so he sat and sat. The spirit of Mara the Tempter appeared to him and tried to break his spiritual composure. Mara tried horrific visions. Mara tried seductive visions. Siddhartha just sat and meditated and paid no mind. And then, one bright morning, he came into the realization of himself as the Buddha, or the Enlightened One. He saw his Original Face. He saw a Golden Embryonic version of himself, with his two inner subtle bodies unified, intertwined within his physical body. He had realized the trikaya and embraced singularity.

The Buddha was thirty-five years old when he reached enlightenment. He spent the remaining forty-five years of his life traveling and preaching his Middle Way, teaching others about the path to enlightenment. His lessons, and the religion that grew beyond his lifetime, brought information to the world about inner illumination that can be duplicated and followed. He wanted an end to suffering bodies, minds, and spirits. He wanted to bring all humankind to spiritual illumination.

He taught lessons about enlightenment. Many different traditions talk of enlightenment, but the basic Chinese/Indian/Tibetan models are very similar. On a simple level, any kind of experience of oneness with the universe, whether in a Zen monastery or even on a simple walk in the woods, which results in a leap in perception and understanding, is a step toward awakening.

In all cases, enlightenment is the result of full activation of the human brain and the achievement of complete evolution of mind and body. Unifying body, soul, and spirit is the goal. It is a union of opposites that integrates the microcosm of the body with the macrocosm of the universe.

It is this integrated totality that created your conception. The opposites fused at the beginning of life. You can easily understand how close our body-mind connection is by examining a newly forming human being. An embryo is ambiguous in gender and very simple in structure at first. Eventually, the more mature embryo develops more and transforms into specific body systems. But, to start with, the same embryonic tissue provides cells for the brain and for the intestinal system. So as the tissue divides, one part becomes the brain and central nervous system; the other part becomes the intestinal system and, in fact, a second brain. Later in fetal development, the two systems are united by the vagus nerve, which is the longest of all our cranial nerves. It creates a direct connection between the brain and gut. The mind runs all through every tissue of our body and our intestines have a primitive connection to the brain.

So you can see that the mind is not just in the brain. Your gut feelings may have more truth than you thought. You may have a sleeping genius within your belly. The scientific discovery of a second brain corresponds with the idea of dormant energy located in the lower torso of the Chinese and Indian medical systems, which results in superconsciousness when fully activated.

Then it also makes perfect sense that a healthy intestinal system, which is one of our goals for good physical health, has a direct influence on how well we think and feel. You will find that Eastern medical systems pay close attention to nutrition and intestinal health. Many natural healing practices consider the belly area to be an energy center. In the chakra system in India, the belly region is the power center, although its source derives from the sexual center below it. Chinese martial arts such as tai chi, as well as qi gong, focus on the lower abdomen as a source of life energy and good health. If you have practiced these gentle arts, you would have heard of the dan tian, a center for developing higher consciousness located below the navel. Complete activation of the energy in the lower torso using systems of spiritual self cultivation such as yoga can result in superconsciousness in humans.

Just as intestines and brain were once all one in the moment of conception, the subtle bodies described in Tantric Buddhism were at one time fully united. Your true self was whole in the beginning of your life. Enlightenment is an attempt to rediscover your true self, this combination, by reuniting the spirit or energy that defined you before birth with the post-birth energy or qi that you experience in life.

Certainly the Buddhists who spoke of trikaya had experience of that union and recognized that the deepest level of ourselves is still whole.

And, although scientists like Alfred Whitehead and Albert Einstein appreciated spirit and spiritual qualities, the consensus reality, and the modern society and culture created by science (scientism) view spiritual illumination with extreme skepticism.

Spirit is a quality that appears, at first glance, to be beyond the scope of the scientific method. Subtle body frameworks are not part of general scientific discussion. But some would say that spirit and soul may be differentiated in that spirit is surely the stuff of soul, but a soul has individuality and identity.

Many lively discussions have centered on these concepts. Western minds as far back as the philosopher Aristotle argued that the spirit and body of a man were separate. It was Rene Descartes who posited, "I think, therefore I am," further helping to segregate the mind from the body.

The rigid structure of Judeo-Christian tradition bred in its practitioners a sense of separation of body and soul. Mind and spirit were bred in the body, but the body was part of a debased and corrupt nature, uninhabited by any God or any higher purpose. Nature and the body were breeding grounds for souls, a predicament rather than

31

anything permanent. A soul's purpose was to look upward toward the higher planes as directed by God, not below to the needs of the mere physical. Death of the body liberated a soul to ascend to a plane of pure spiritual beings.

At the extremes of this philosophy, ascetics mortified their bodies by fasting or even flagellating themselves in order to further divide the pure spirit from the disgusting mortal coil to which it was bound.

On the other side of the coin, however, was the resultant materialism. Not the actual thought-out philosophy begun by certain Greek philosophers maintaining that only matter matters, but rather, the preoccupation with material things as a cultural and social trend. It seems that many people just ignore their spiritual life; it is something of no concern until close to the time of death when it finally develops importance. Most of life, for many people, is about possessions and the wanting and the getting of them. Buying and selling becomes a substitute for real meaning.

However, people are beginning to be influenced by the spiritual concepts brought from the Eastern traditions. They provide a satisfying combination of spirituality and science. Buddhism, when observed in the way it was created, is not just a belief system, but includes a scientific tradition. Actually, Siddhartha was just one of many Buddhas, and according to tradition, should not be worshipped as a deity. His image is a reminder to be venerated, perhaps, but is not an idol because the idea is that all of us can reach Buddhahood. We can all be Buddhas. The deepest level of ourselves has always been the state of enlightenment.

All of the techniques to attain unity of body/soul/spirit are available to learn; including meditation, tai chi, qi gong, and various types of yoga. All can be practiced now, to produce various levels of remarkable effects. And along the way, the journey to enlightenment has the immediate gifts of better health and happiness, and increased longevity.

Your true nature can be revealed with spiritual awakening, bringing to you a complete awareness of your true self, your Original Face, the Spiritual Embryo. The truth of science and religion in a combined system, such as those brought to us from Eastern spiritual/medical teachers, opens to us the view of our ultimate potential. You can rediscover your original primordial reality, which is enlightenment, the ultimate evolution of human mind and body.

KEY CONCEPTS

- The trikaya is the conjunction of physical and subtle bodies achievable through defined practices – such as various inner yogas, meditation, tai chi, and qi gong – learned from Eastern traditions that combined science and religion, such as Tantric Buddhism and Chinese Medicine.
- Buddhism is a science of consciousness begun by Prince Siddhartha, who saw his Original Face and spent his remaining days teaching the methods toward that goal.
- The trikaya represents complete matter, energy and information, symmetry, total consciousness unification, the perfect integration that enables us to realize enlightenment or Buddhahood.
- The trikaya represents complete evolution of the human mind and body.
- The source of our selves has always been spiritually whole and enlightened.
- The scientific discovery of a second brain in the intestinal tissue corresponds with the concept of a dormant enlightened energy in the lower torso of the body in Chinese and Indian medical systems.
- Enlightenment can be said to result from full activation of the human brain and the achievement of complete evolution of mind and body.
- The union of our inner subtle bodies fully connects us with the universe.
- The starting point of the human body is the enlightened origin of ourselves.

CHAPTER SIX
Rocks Can Change Your Mind

It is a mark of an educated mind to be able to entertain a thought without accepting it.
Aristotle

So as you explore new ideas within Eastern thought, you can at least consider the possibilities. Really, when you think about it, what is real?

In his biography of the famous British lexicographer Dr. Samuel Johnson, James Boswell tells the story of a discussion between himself and Johnson concerning the philosophical theories of Bishop Berkeley. The Bishop suggested that matter wasn't real, but a reflection of ideals. Dr. Johnson became so infuriated with the idea he stepped forward and kicked a rock in front of them. "I refute it thus!" he cried angrily.

Who is correct? Everything we look at depends upon assumptions. New information can refute or support assumptions. If what we look at can change with additional information, then what we see is an illusion based on perceptions. Ultimate mental freedom allows us to be able to rethink our reality.

A rock is not always a rock. To a hunter, it might be a weapon for throwing and killing prey. To a camper, it might be a tool to drive in a tent stake. To a child, a rock may be a plaything for skipping across a pond or to hit with a stick. To a geologist, a rock holds the story of earth; tales of fire or water or immense pressures. To a chemist, a rock is a combination of elements. To a physicist, it is a collection of atoms with more gaps than solid particles. To a jeweler, it can be a source of beauty. Now we can look at a rock with more perspective, we have opened our minds. Opening our mind opens the doors for a multitude of possibilities.

Our minds hold us in traditional illusions of reality. Breaking free of illusion allows us to accept the concept that we are capable of a multitude of possibilities. This is spiritual and mental freedom. When we seek enlightenment, we look for the source of our self, our true nature, among all these possibilities.

Our reality can change. Our thoughts and energy can change our mind and body for the better. We all have within us the ultimate potential for Buddhahood. We can all be enlightened. We can all achieve immortality. We, who are made up of atoms, chemicals, and physiological systems, are so much more than just living cells. We have the potential to change our body and mind to fully evolve in just one lifetime and become one with the universe.

We have seen the evidence of how we can use our minds to change our physical health. One third of all healing is attributed to the placebo effect. Research on new medical drugs typically uses a double blind experiment in which half the people are given the new drug and half are given a placebo, a harmless non-medicinal substance. Neither the medical team giving the pills nor the people swallowing the pills know which half of the study group they are in. These studies have often had the surprising result that the person taking the placebo, the "sugar pill," has just as good a result, or even better than the new pharmaceutical substance being tested. The placebo works because it is the thought that healing will occur that is the actual cure.

An interesting note here is that science and medicine may use the term placebo in a derogative way, but the placebo effect represents the natural healing ability of the mind/body continuum and the power of the mind to balance and heal the body.

You may have heard of people who made an appointment to see their doctor with a painful condition and feel embarrassed because as soon as they made the appointment or when they arrived at the doctor's office, the pain subsided. The healing process began with the belief that healing would occur.

Like the rock that Dr. Johnson kicked, most of us are locked in the illusion that reality creates consciousness. A mind is said to be a construct of the body, time and experience. In truth it is the lens of consciousness.

As conscious human beings, we are aware. We do more than notice the smell of fresh mown grass, the sight of a spectacularly colorful sunset, the softness of a kitten, the sour taste of a dill pickle, or the sound of rain pounding against a window. We also have the added awareness of being aware of our awareness. We are aware of our consciousness.

Evidence suggests that consciousness is a form of information. Scientists understand information. It can be measured. It can be replicated. It can be categorized. Formulas can be created to understand, describe, and verify truth. Both consciousness and information can be increased. We begin to see that consciousness creates reality.

The famous cancer researcher, Candace Pert, Ph.D., also explains the physiology of the mind-body connection in her book, *Molecules of*

Emotion. [3] This very close mind-body connection that formed within the embryo works at the cellular level. Dr. Pert explains the biomolecular basis for our emotions. Her discovery of the opiate receptor fueled the synthesis of behavior, psychology, and biology. She pioneered research on how the chemicals inside our bodies form a dynamic information network, linking mind and body. Her work was at the forefront of the new interdisciplinary field, psychoneuroimmunology, that studies integrated mind-body solutions in relationship to the immune system. Dr. Pert personally believes in the power of meditation.

We already know we can use the mind to change the brain. Take a look at the field of hypnotherapy.

Hypnosis has the potential to accelerate the healing process of both the mind and the body. Its power is seen in the wide variety of issues that respond well to hypnosis, such as: general anxiety, insomnia, compulsion, decision making, confidence, self acceptance, test anxiety, smoking abstinence, procrastination, pain management, improved immune system, enhanced athletic performance, weight loss, phobias, and recovery support from addiction. Hypnosis can also be a means for achieving higher consciousness or higher human potential in terms of mind/body evolution.

Hypnosis is safe and effective when done within a professional therapeutic relationship. Ethical Ericksonian techniques ensure that the client is in control and aware at all times. The client is guided within a personally designed scenario. A trained therapist is valuable but not necessary and the therapist does not actually have to be present; you can use a tape with visual imagery appropriate for your goal or made specifically for you. You can also use a person playing therapist-surrogate, reading from a script.

Hypnosis works because much of your perception is subconsciously organized. Progressive relaxation techniques, in a trusting environment, allow you to bypass your conscious mind and tap into the subconscious. By working in your subconscious territory and breaking through your cultural "programming" with suggestions and hypnotic techniques, you can break down the walls of illusion that the conscious mind has built. All those defensive thoughts and mechanisms are bypassed so that your true self is allowed to rule your beliefs and actions. You can break down the illusions of your reality and break through into deeper levels of awareness.

3 *Molecules of Emotion, The Science Behind Mind-Body Medicine by* Candace Pert, Scribner, 1997.

There isn't a consensus of opinion on what hypnosis is in the medical community. However, it has been proven that hypnosis has powerful mind-body effects. Under suggestion, when touched by an ice cube and told it is a lit cigarette tip, a red welt can appear on the individual's skin as if they had actually been burned. The mind does not distinguish between mental and physical states at deeper levels.

Hypnosis taps into the powerful link between the mind and the body. If used correctly, hypnosis can allow a person to achieve advanced meditation skills and to transcend the barriers of space and time imposed by the consensus reality created by culture and society. Even a simple self-hypnosis suggestion serves well.

In the early 20th century, a psychologist named Emile Coue taught hundreds of thousands of people a simple phrase. "Every day in every way, I am getting better and better." He gave a simple prescription for a better life, including the curing of serious medical conditions. He said to repeat this phrase over and over, especially at bedtime, just before sleep and just after waking. Despite controversy, thousands of people benefited from this form of auto suggestion.

Along the powerful lines of body-mind integration, you may be asking yourself how this applies to your growth in terms of spiritual awakening.

Suppose you said to yourself, "Every day in every way I am getting more and more enlightened".

Could this actually help bring you closer to enlightenment? Yes. Emphatically. You just have to remember to do it.

How does this work? Scientists now know that neurotransmitters in our brains are involved in a dynamic information network, linking our thoughts and physical processes. They have found the links between mind and body.

J. D. Bekenstein, in 2003, pointed out the growing trend in physics to define the physical world as being made of information. So you could look at a rock and see it as a chunk of information. A rock is a geological statement, a chemical statement, a dynamic clump of molecules held together by laws of attraction.

Rocks don't change much. They break apart and wear down by erosion; they get moved around by waves, machines, and earthquakes.

But minds change. The information in our brain changes because we are capable of absorbing new information. The part of our brain that is overexcited or underactive can be changed by chemicals, drugs,

37

cognitive behavioral therapy that addresses thinking errors, or just by simply practicing positive thoughts.

Yes, concentrated positive thoughts can change the brain.

Ready for another rock story?

There once was a Tibetan monk who started each morning meditation by sitting between two piles of rocks; one black and one white. Whenever he had a negative thought, he put one black rock in front of him and when he had a positive thought he put one white rock in the same pile. When he first started practicing this way, he would end his meditation and find a mixed pile of white and black rocks. A long meditation filled with negative thoughts could have made his life worse, putting too much emphasis on anger, frustration, and disappointments. He knew that working on positive thinking would be beneficial, creating a healthier mind. A healthy mind would support his spiritual practice and bring him closer to enlightenment. Progress depended on him implementing the golden rule, "do unto others as you would have them do unto you", in all states of consciousness, at all times. He accepted the ideal, to seek to always benefit all sentient beings and reduce the harm to all sentient beings. He knew that generating a negative thought or behaving negatively were actions damaging to his own being. A positive thought generated is a benefit. It is the goal of enlightenment to be, at all times, one with the universe, at which point you are naturally in accord with all things. He wanted to achieve enlightenment so that he could benefit and enable all others to achieve enlightenment, the goal of the bodhisattva warrior.

So gradually, he worked every day on refining his thoughts. Eventually, his meditation would end with only white rocks in his pile. That is the essence of spiritual practice, to attain a goal that brings your life closer to perfection.

On the other hand, negative thoughts and negative emotions prevent smooth harmonious cultivation. Negative thoughts and emotions are unhealthy. Steroid-induced rage in athletes is a prime example of a harmful effect of hormone enhancement because it artificially increases energy with an out of control effect. If you are very sad or very angry it would be hard to get into a true qi state, which is actually a hypnotic relaxation trance state, similar to the state between sleeping and wakening. An angry person would have to be much calmer and would need her blood pressure to go down. If negative emotions evoke irregular or unnatural breathing patterns, then lengthening, deepening, and slowing breathing should result in a calmer person. The deeper you can go into a deep sleeplike trance state while in meditation, the more natural qi is generated. If your qi is strong and balanced, you should have more positive thoughts and positive emotions. The Buddhist belief is that the mind rides on the qi or prana. If qi is calm then the mind is calm. It is important to take negative thoughts and emotions and transform them into positive thoughts and emotions.

Another example to look at is depression, which is a lack of vitality along with negative thoughts. If you are depressed, you could elevate your mood by increasing the vitality of your body, which then energizes your mind. With more qi, or vitality, a person can be more positive. Healthy practices that increase the amount of physical exercise, fresh air, good sleep, and positive thoughts are helpful. If your qi is strong, you can feel better; if your qi is weak you are going to feel low. Good meditation generates greater levels of qi, along with practices of physical techniques such as tai chi, qi gong, and yoga.

Slow and deep natural breathing techniques taught specifically for that purpose will enhance your qi cultivation. In essence, you go back to breathing the way you were breathing when you were still inside your mother. Harnessing the original qi of the body, which is always enlightened and still connected to Tao or the universe, brings powerful and healthy effects and greater potential.

We are all capable of finding our own special powers. We can consistently work on achieving greater and greater levels of potential by generating positive energy and positive thoughts. We can do this with effective breathing techniques, correct meditation and physical techniques. In the end, we create greater health, wisdom, and longevity by strengthening the connection of our mind-body energy with nature and the universe.

Physicists and spiritual seekers see that there is some force, some natural laws, that attract various particles and create every substance known to us. And we know that we can change the health of our bodies just by investing our time in more positive thinking. So we can begin to see how the quality of our consciousness changes the whole system of body-mind-spirit. The trikaya of complete unification of body, spirit, and soul creates a perfection of being.

The next frontiers for Western science may very well be the discovery of the links to spirit. Like human eyes, human spirit often does not see itself. It is inevitable that the future will see neuroscientists studying enlightenment, the source of self. Eventually, they will find the Golden Embryonic answer, the most ancient secret of Chinese medicine. Matter is spirit dreaming in the bed of mind.

KEY CONCEPTS
- What we look at, our reality, is based on assumptions. Our reality is an illusion.
- Spiritual freedom comes from breaking through illusions. Ultimate mental freedom allows us to be able to rethink our reality.
- Our reality can change. The placebo effect and hypnosis are examples of how we can use our minds to accelerate the healing process of both mind and body.
- Scientists found that neurotransmitters in our brains link our thoughts and physical processes within a dynamic information network.
- We can create greater health, wisdom, and longevity by strengthening the connection of our mind-body energy with nature and the universe.
- We are capable of a multitude of possibilities. When we seek enlightenment, we look for the source of our self, our true nature, among all those possibilities.
- We have the potential to change our body and mind to fully evolve in just one lifetime and become one with the universe.
- Reality does not create consciousness. Consciousness creates reality–and then gets distracted.
- Neuroscientists studying the source of self will eventually find the Golden Embryonic answer, the most ancient secret of Chinese medicine.

CHAPTER SEVEN
The Philosopher's Stone:
The Missing Link of Alchemy

A human being is a luminous field of complete and perfect awareness and has the potential to reunite with the universal mind. This universal mind, or the void, is the source of reality.

The above idea is not a part of Western culture, a culture where science and spirituality run in separate circles, which is ironic because perhaps the scientist who had the greatest impact on the modern world was also a man who did not separate his faith from his work.

This scientist was Sir Isaac Newton and he was an alchemist.

You may know of him from the Disney version of the history of science. Isaac Newton is the guy in the funny-looking wig, getting conked on the noggin when an apple falls from a tree. He analyzes the incident and discovers the law of gravity. Animations of equations rise up in cartoon land, turning into rockets traveling to the moon and the joyful physics of Tomorrowland.

The cartoon is actually based on a real story, as fantasy so often is. Newton did tell a story about watching an apple's fall from a tree. William Stukeley immortalized the conversation with Newton in Kensington, England on April 15, 1726, in his *Memoirs of Sir Isaac Newton*. Stukeley said that his friend told him that the observation of an apple's fall from a tree opened an awareness in him of the force of gravity. Newton had been sitting in a contemplative mood, his mind open. He reported pondering about gravitation after watching the apple fall:

Why should that apple always descend perpendicularly to the ground....Why should it not go sideways or upwards, but constantly to the Earth's centre? Assuredly the reason is, that the Earth draws it. There must be a drawing power in matter. And the sum of the drawing power in the matter of the Earth must be in the Earth's centre, not in any side of the Earth. Therefore does this apple fall perpendicularly or towards the centre? If matter thus draws matter; it must be proportion of its quantity. Therefore the apple draws the Earth, as well as the Earth draws the apple.

These were mighty thoughts indeed, but not surprising coming from Newton, who was a highly respected scientist, theologian, alchemist, philosopher, astronomer, physicist, and mathematician. His contributions to humankind are held in the highest respect to this day and there were many you would recognize. Newton shares credit for developing differential and integral calculus and studied the speed of sound. He made the final and conclusive argument for the planetary movements that proved the earth was not the center of the universe. He developed a theory of color using prisms to break down white light into the visible spectrum. He built the first reflective telescope and described three laws of motion:

(1) law of inertia: an object at rest tends to stay at rest and an object in uniform motion tends to stay in uniform motion unless acted upon by a net external force.

(2) law of acceleration: an applied force on an object equals the rate of change of its momentum with time.

(3) law of relativity: every action creates an equal and opposite reaction.

Interestingly, Newton's work was done just decades from Galileo's day in Papal Court. And while Newton staunchly believed in a theistic God, his views on the Trinity would have landed him in hot water with the clerics in charge at his home college in Cambridge, England.

Isaac Newton simply did not believe that Jesus was God's equal and thus he was not a Trinitarian. Yet, Newton was highly religious and studied the Holy Bible prodigiously and famously concluded:

Gravity explains the motions of the planets, but it cannot explain who set the planets in motion. God governs all things and knows all that is or can be done.

Newton's God was a distant God who challenged humankind with a basket of mysteries to muddle through. Newton dove into that basket of mysteries with astounding energy. He used the clarity and simplicity of science to answer both the superlatives of overenthusiastic religious people and the accusations of superstition put forth by atheists.

Although he was maybe best remembered as a famous mathematician and scientist, evidence exists that Newton spent far more time and energy on his Bible and alchemy than in founding the basics of modern physics.

It may be that his work was intentionally hidden. He wrote over a million words on alchemy. But after his death in 1727, the Royal Society decided his work on the subject was not a fit subject for printing. Another possibility was that he kept his work private to maintain some sort of noble "high silence". What we do know is that his lost work was rediscovered in the mid-twentieth century. It became apparent to the scholars who read his alchemical studies that this work may well have been the inspiration for his conception of laws about light and gravity.

As a practicing alchemist, Newton spent days locked up in his laboratory, and many people believe he finally succeeded in transmuting lead into gold. When he died in his eighties, it was discovered his body was riddled with mercury from his experiments. Perhaps that explains one of the oddest things about his life. At the height of his career, instead of accepting a professorship at Cambridge, he was appointed Director of the Royal Mint with the responsibility of securing and accounting for England's repository of gold. As a warden of the English Royal Mint, he reported that 20 per cent of the coinage was counterfeit. True to his scientific nature, Newton disguised himself as a frequenter of bars to gather proof. He worked at prosecuting coiners of counterfeit money and proposed a plan for the Royal Mint to produce coinage that could not be counterfeited. But his passion for alchemy, the beginning of modern chemistry, went beyond mundane experiments with natural elements.

Newton considered alchemy to be a real science, as much as his other studies. But not just the beginnings of chemistry – putting different substances together to see the effect – he saw alchemy as a link between matter, soul and spirit.

Yes, Newton's alchemy was more than just about turning lead into gold or finding the magic elixir of life and immortality, the Philosopher's Stone (the name given to a substance believed by medieval alchemists to have the power to change base metals into gold or silver). The Philosopher's Stone, according to some, had the power of prolonging life and of curing all injuries and diseases. The pursuit of it by alchemists led to the discovery of several chemical substances.

If this magic elixir sounds oddly familiar, you may be thinking of J. K. Rowling's first book, Harry Potter and the Sorcerer's Stone. Indeed, in the original version, it was called Harry Potter and the Philosopher's Stone. An editorial decision changed the title to make it more appealing for children. In the book, the secret power of the stone was immortality, sought by the dark wizard, Voldemort, who used unicorn's blood to maintain a wisp of existence, a half life, until he could steal the elixir of eternal life. The stone was hidden deep inside Hogwarts, the wizardry school, with a ferocious beast as its guard.

However, the fabled stone wasn't meant to be found in a treasure chest or any other hidden location. In fact it wasn't even actually a stone. There was no rock. It was a metaphor for the sacred combination that brings immortality. The real Philosopher's Stone is the starting point of the body. Newton's alchemical work contained the seeds for understanding what we seek in our journey from matter to spirit, from human body to the doors of perception for the human race.

The Philosopher's Stone

Here is a 17th *century illustration of the spiritual embryo as the philosopher's stone within the lower abdomen of the alchemist. M Maire, Atalanta fugiens, Oppenheim, 1618.*

Western alchemy had a strong connection with the philosophical and spiritual system called Hermeticism. Hermes Trismegistus was an alchemist of Egyptian-Greek origins whose name means "thrice-blessed." He is credited with writings and practices of applied philosophy and inquiry into the nature of the universe. Most particularly, alchemists focused on Hermes' discussion of what was termed The Operation of the Sun. This alchemical work sought not to turn lead into gold; rather, it was about how a person seeks to transform themselves from a base person, symbolized by lead, into an adept master, symbolized by gold. The various stages of chemical distillation and fermentation are symbolic metaphors of the Magnum Opus, or Great Work, performed on the soul.

Newton was committed to the notion of the Hermetic tradition, a body of alchemical knowledge that extended back to ancient times. His interest led him to translate the Emerald Tablet of Hermes Trismegistus, to look for alchemical instructions, the formula for the Philosopher's Stone.

Western souls have not just been searching for spiritual truths through conceptual means. As with the Tantric Buddhist concept of trikaya, Western alchemists searched for an answer that would result in a physical transformation that unified mind, body and spirit. The search was for the combination that would lead to a sacred unity, a Western version of the trikaya.

Alchemy is a complex spiritual exercise, utilizing matter. It is held secret in the spiritual disciplines of many ancient civilizations. It has inner and outer branches. In the East, alchemy's adherents to inner disciplines sought to activate the kundalini, an essential spiritual energy in the human body. Practitioners of the outer branches of alchemy in the East were, and continue to be, concerned with refining medicinal substances in order to achieve greater health and longevity.

In its broadest definition, alchemy not only looked into the working of matter in Nature, but was a discipline of the spirit, a philosophy. Its roots and branches reached into all ancient scientific work – stretching into medicine, astrology, art and symbology – unifying them all into a single force. Alchemical schools and philosophical systems were active, as near as records can tell, for nearly three thousand years, stretching back to ancient Egypt, Mesopotamia, Persia, India, China, Classical Rome, Greece and all Muslim civilizations, and then actively in Europe up to the nineteenth century. Full-blown traditional Western alchemists still practice today, although far more obscurely.

As Richard Smoley and Jay Kinney point out in their survey of Western esoteric traditions, *Hidden Wisdom*[4], we need to look at two fundamental principles of alchemy or hermetic science, sol and luna. Sol is sun, gold, heaven, light. Luna is moon, silver, water, stone,

4 *Hidden Wisdom* by Richard Smoley and Jay Kinney, Penguin, 2006.

ocean, night and more. Said Cornelius Agrippa, "No one can excel in the alchemical art without knowing these principles in himself; and the greater the knowledge of self, the greater will be the magnetic power attained thereby and the greater the wonders to be realized."

Gold represents superconsciousness, enlightenment or the ultimate perfection of the soul by uniting it with the original spirit within the physical body – corpus, anima and spiritus.

Alchemical texts are intentional concoctions of mysterious metaphors, a twilight language. Remember how Galileo created a stir with the Church? Sir Isaac Newton would have been in a lot of trouble with the church powers if they understood what he was truly up to. Considering the Catholic Church's burn-first-and-ask-questions-later attitude to the Cathars and anyone at all they dubbed as heretics, it was prudent to write a lyrical version of the alchemical process and its underlying intention.

In the Middle Ages and a long time after the time when Western alchemy operated, ideas that opposed the ideas of the Church were dangerous. By cloaking these ideas in symbols and metaphor, alchemists could not only pass along knowledge and ideas, but also prevent any frocked eyes from understanding the true nature of their work.

This echoes the concept of the Holy Grail as revealed in Dan Brown's *The Da Vinci Code*. Rather than a golden goblet, his grail was a symbol representing the repressed Divine Feminine aspect of Christianity. The cup was symbolic of a female vessel. Both the Philosopher's Stone and the Holy Grail were thus visual symbols of an unseen superpower.

Alchemy was a work of the synthesis of matter, mind and spirit, a tapestry of evolving imagination and material poetry, encoded to be reproduced. In other words, the alchemists would seem to be creating what we might consider the very stuff of superconsciousness, a system of enlightened information.

Whether or not any alchemist actually was able to come up with a substance that would turn lead into gold doesn't really matter. The term Philosopher's Stone represents something vital to human existence, the starting point of the body, transformed into the golden face of God within one's self, the real you.

The Philosopher's Stone's matter is planted equally in the human body, the human mind, and the human spirit. It is the path, the doorway through the material of this trinity toward something that is often called salvation in the West and enlightenment in the East. It's the doorway to where we want to go. And the doorway isn't beyond us, it's in us. Just as the whole universe is in us.

> To see a World in a Grain of Sand
> And a Heaven in a Wild Flower,
> Hold Infinity in the palm of your hand
> And Eternity in an hour.

That's a quote from the visionary poet William Blake, and it's a good jumping point from which to discuss another concept of alchemy, whose truth echoes through both spiritual and scientific inquiries through the ages and around the world.

Just as in alchemy, molecular biology and quantum physics, Blake speaks of a microcosm and a macrocosm, a small ordered world and a large ordered world

Although thanks to sophisticated telescopes we can see deep into the cosmos, most of what we know about the universe comes from our experience and experiments on the planet Earth. It follows that we can say that Earth is a microcosm of the universe, the macrocosm.

We can also think in terms of patterns or paradigms. The best example of this kind of pattern is DNA, the genetic code for living beings. From a single sample from one sheep, biologists were able to clone another sheep. In every cell of your body lies the code, the information that can recreate another you.

Alchemy was useful in structuring patterns of matter, utilizing the tools of the mind, after the observed and experienced properties of the spirit's impact on both.

Pythagoras discovered the Golden Ratio and its philosophical product, the Golden Mean. As stated by Aristotle, the Golden Mean is the desirable middle between two extremes. The Greeks sought a rational explanation for everything, and noticed repetition of patterns. The Golden Mean and the Golden Ratio could be discerned as patterns here on Earth. Why not the entire cosmos? Could they be smaller versions of larger patterns? It was a useful way of looking at reality, and certainly a foundation of modern science.

Alchemy attempted to access the macrocosm of spiritual truths, through the microcosm of present materials. Thus alchemists connected their work with the microcosm and macrocosm directly with the human body. In the human body the microcosm is the starting point, a point which represents totality, the whole. In a cosmic sense, we transform soul to gold. The human body mirrors the whole universe. The human is also the pivot between higher and lower dimensions of heaven and earth. When a human is enlightened the dimensions are united. Pure consciousness, heaven, being at one with the universe, unites the microcosm and macrocosm.

A junction of opposites such as heaven and earth unites micro and macro. A cosmic union of mother and son lights reunites spirit with itself. As a child runs and embraces its mother so the soul embraces the spirit. The Chinese goal of alchemy and medicine is to see the Golden Embryo, perfecting the soul. When ones sees the Golden Embryo, the third eye opens and then dormant memory comes back with realization of divine being, and one becomes a living Buddha or sage, gains spiritual freedom, and achieves the trikaya. The Philosopher's Stone is more valuable than anything on earth. It represents finding immortality or Buddhahood. The alchemical discovery is that the universe is holographic and is contained within the body, which contains all information. The whole being is within the part, so the part has all the information within it to create the universe. It is but an illusion that body and universe are separate. Each creates the other, united by the mind. The one is the many. The many are one.

Symbols of this union are in evidence throughout world cultures. The holy spirit of Christianity represents three bodies in one. The Philosopher's Stone is represented as a hermetic androgyne, half male and half female, in a single body. The serpent swallowing its tail is the most ancient symbol of alchemy.

Other cultures refer to inner gold, or a golden statue wrapped in dirty rags, or the golden treasure under the floor. The Philosopher's Stone is variously referred to in other teachings as the Hermetic Androgyne, the Golden Elixir, the Prima Materia, the Vajra Bindu, the Immortal Drop, the Golden Flower, Kundalini, Rebis, the Holy Spirit, Tathagatagharba, the Spiritual Fetus, the Immortal Embryo, and the Original Face.

Perhaps we can use some of the ideas and terms of alchemy to help guide the Western mind through a journey that threads through body, mind and spirit, and binds them fast.

For the most part, our culture does not have the idea of activating the starting point of the body and using it to supercharge the brain. We've lost the idea of the Philosopher's Stone, the Golden Embryonic version of ourself.

KEY CONCEPTS

- Sir Isaac Newton studied both science and religion with equal intensity.
- Newton was a devoted alchemist whose studies on the subject were copious and largely forgotten until recently.
- Alchemy is a parent to modern science, but in fact is a science of body, mind and spirit.
- The key concept of Alchemy is the Philosopher's Stone, a metaphor for the intersection of body, mind and spirit.
- The Philosopher's Stone is the starting point of the body, sourced in spirit.
- Immortality is achieved through fusion of opposites by heating up the starting point of the body using breathing, meditation, yoga, tai chi, qi gong or sexual yoga.
- The concept of the Philosopher's Stone is echoed in other spiritual systems, under other names.
- The Philosopher's Stone is a Golden Embryonic version of yourself.

CHAPTER EIGHT
Kundalini

Inner alchemy was the desired fusion of body, mind and spirit to create spiritual awakening and immortality. That search spanned the centuries and covered the earth for the mystical starting point that would provide inner illumination or enlightenment.

So we join that search as we travel now to India, the land of exotic spices and a spiritual practice called kundalini awakening, to locate the Philosopher's Stone in the body. Amidst this country with its enticing scents of curry we are not surprised to find a spiritual fusion, because curry is a mix of opposites, a blend of sweet and savory. Ayurveda is the Hindu science of medicine and ancient Sanskrit writings tell of medicinal uses of spices: pepper for digestive ailments, ginger for liver complaints and rheumatism, cardamom for headaches, coriander for constipation, cloves for brain ailments.

Ancient cooks combined ayurvedic knowledge with a refined sense of smell and taste to create an art form of combining spices. Although you may find curry in the spice section of your favorite grocery store, Indian curry was literally a sauce made with a combination of sweet and savory spices; blending cumin, turmeric, pepper, coriander, fenugreek, ginger, garlic, cinnamon, mustard, cardamom, clove, nutmeg, and fennel seed. The scents of Indian cooking enliven the nose while eating Indian dishes enhance the digestive system, and build immunity of the whole body.

Ancient practices of kundalini yoga point to the starting point of the body, the interface of body, soul, and spirit. The process of kundalini awakening involves moving energy to awaken consciousness, to discover your true self.

In Western Alchemy, manipulation of matter was also a process. Alchemists were dealing with matter, but they knew as well as we do that our bodies are composed of matter, segmented into specialized and integrated systems.

Sensory organs, for instance, allow us to hear through our ears, smell though our noses and see through our eyes. Our organs are in predictable places, organized by the information of our genetic code. Western science has successfully mapped out the physiological processes in the human body.

But to begin a spiritual alchemical process, alchemists wanted to find the exact starting point of the body. They searched for the Philosopher's Stone within the human form, which would unlock the mysteries of the universe.

Starting with a look at the human embryo, we see it goes through various stages of development before it becomes fully human in form. One of the first stages that can be recognized is referred to as reptilian. This is when the reptilian complex of the brain develops, the driving force for the whole organism, with the basic operating system below the larger mammalian section of the brain and the neo-cortex. The reptilian brain consists of the upper part of the spinal cord and the basal ganglia, the diencephalon, and parts of the midbrain. It controls vital functions of the body such as breathing and body temperature, yet it works without conscious effort. One could think of it as the door knob that holds open the door of life, or the head of the serpent; the kundalini energy of the body. Indeed perhaps it is a reminder of an ancient reptilian-mammalian evolutionary link. We know for sure that all mammals living today have this reptilian complex system. The snake resides within us; the serpent lies coiled at the base of our spine. It's energy lies dormant, waiting to be awakened.

Ancient spiritual practices in India tapped into this dormant energy, called kundalini. It is the mysterious energy of the body that brings superpowers to those who activate it. It is a dormant enlightened energy, which resides within the lower torso of the human body and is activated through yogic practice or meditation and results in enlightenment, inner illumination and immortality.

The process was developed through systems of yoga in India in which an inner heat is brought to bear on the lowest chakra.

When we think of yoga, we mostly think of systems of exercise that stretch the body, help us get limber, and calm us down. The success of yoga's work with the body is well documented. A lot of scientists do yoga!

In fact, yoga is a system or exercise that can be documented, learned and repeated – a form of information – to attain not only physical results, but mental and spiritual results. Why is there yoga everywhere now in Western culture? Because it works.

Although like the martial arts in physical and mental results, yoga's systems were developed for spiritual purposes–to find our way to connection with spirit through body and mind, and to forge that trikaya.

Where is the Philosopher's Stone in all this?

Well, the Indian masters thought of it as the Golden Serpent lying coiled, sleeping or perhaps even hibernating at the base of one's spine.

This is what is called kundalini, a psycho-spiritual force, the energy of superconsciousness. The ancient masters claimed to have discovered this kind of corporeal energy in the sacrum or base of the spine. Their energy system flowed through chakras.

The chakras are perceived as energy centers which correspond to places or points on the human body serving as spiritual wheels, drawn as lotus flowers with varying numbers of petals. They occur along the spine and usually correspond to what are known in the West as major nerve ganglia, such as the third chakra's location at the solar plexus and the sixth chakra's location at the pineal gland.

We've suggested here that there are portals to spirit in the body. In India, as you can see by the illustration, these were mapped out. The benefits of accessing these energy points at the most surface level allows us to ease the toll of modern life on our bodies. Yoga exercises reward their performers with that golden goal of modern society: relaxation, and a relief from unhealthy stress. Bliss, vitality, and health are proven results.

Yet, in the most ancient secret of yoga, the stored energy in the lower torso, when fully activated and raised to the top of the head, results in enlightenment or immortality.

The seven layers of manifestation of this kundalini energy are said to form a rainbow bridge, connecting heaven and earth, stepping stones from matter to spirit. We have the potential to connect our bodies to the source of all life, ever awakening into higher consciousness. Along a central channel from base to crown, energy spins at these intersections from basic currents coming from above and simultaneously from below. Together, the seven chakras are said to describe a formula for wholeness.

As shown in the illustration, the location of the chakras logically incorporates their meaning.

The first chakra, known as the root chakra, is located at the base of the spine. It represents the material world, the force that binds energy to form, the density of the physical world. Its element is earth, and it is connected to our survival instinct, our primal energy, and our connection to earth's matrix. Ancient Indian spiritual beliefs describe the serpentine energy of the goddess kundalini Shakti that lies dormant at this base chakra. When aroused through inner heating, it journeys up the spine until it reaches the crown at the top of the skull. When the energy returns to the root chakra, it finds support, deep in the earth. Here you return home, to the peace, stillness, and solidity of the natural world.

Seven Power Centers or Chakras of the Kundalini System

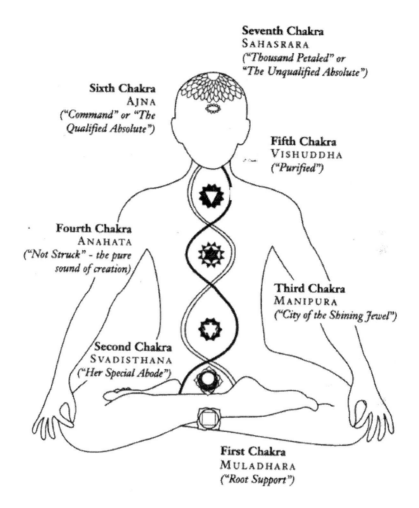

*Wheels of Life – Seven Power Centers or Chakras
of the Kundalini System*

*The chakras are depicted as lotuses. The spirals indicate the contrasting
energies of psyche and spirit: the fiery energy and darker helix contrast with the
lighter, spiritual energies and lighter helix, all of which must be brought together in
balance.*
*Joseph Campbell, The Mythic Image (Princeton, N.J.) Princeton
University Press, 1974.*

The second chakra is related to water, as it contains the continuing ebb and flow of duality, opposites attracting, moving and flowing toward each other with primal longing to merge together as one. In this chakra you experience desires, dividing and uniting. Thus it creates the eternal yin/yang of existence. It is located in the sacrum, hips, and pelvis; the seat of movement, sensation, pleasure, and desire. As two become one in ecstatic embrace, it is satisfied, having danced in the waters of duality and sent its energy upward.

Moving to the third chakra, located at the solar plexus, kundalini takes on the element of fire. Here you are a vitalized being, with energy, power, strength, will and purpose. Here you can burn through blocks to greater freedom and power, beyond the ego. Igniting the energy, the fiery serpent of kundalini harnesses energy from the belly and sends it to the next level.

The fourth chakra is the heart chakra. Like the air element, it brings the spaciousness of sky, and with the soft wings of love it brings energy upward with each breath. It creates spaciousness within, uniting heaven and earth, mind and body, male and female with compassion and love.

Rising up to the fifth chakra, the throat chakra represents purification, an etheric realm. Here vibrations are awakened, sound stirs on the air of breath. The murmur of voice is now within, a song rising from the heart, from the primordial Om, the first sound of creation.

At the sixth chakra located midcenter in the brow, kundalini is now a glowing serpent of light charged to open the third eye, a center of vision and insight. It is represented by two lotus petals, the resolution of duality to the single point of focus of the third eye, which sees the radiant light within. It sees the Golden Embryo and recognizes the Original Face. Waves of awareness pierce through illusion and bring clarity. As the third eye opens between two physical eyes, it opens an inner portal as illumination unfolds within the mind's eye.

Finally at the seventh chakra, the crown chakra at the top of the head, the serpent pierces the crown. The crown chakra is represented by the thousandfold lotus, fully complete, blossoming with infinite awareness from consciousness within. It is awake, aware and intelligent, divine, ever unfolding into infinite awareness. A still mind may witness sparks of illumination as the goddess Shakti meets her divine consort Shiva. Shiva then gives birth to stars, a journey to the heart of the cosmos and intelligent creation, the divine mind, a universal consciousness that is the source of all.

All are enlightened and united from base to crown, energized, fully illuminated through this ancient Indian yogic technique.

Is this our Philosopher's Stone?

The fusion seems right. Corporeal energy is exactly our base of operations for this inquiry. The principal of kundalini is strong, it's impact on record. Activating one's kundalini is said to cause a tremendous increase in the energy level of the human body, which, when properly channeled, results in a higher level of mental and physical performance as well as greatly heightened powers of perception.

A warning: kundalini is powerful energy and needs to be accessed carefully with proper training from a master. Untrained or unmonitored practitioners have been known to have experienced psychotic episodes or even physical breakdowns from unwise activation, too much too fast. The original goal of yoga is to strengthen the body to withstand the power of the kundalini.

Modern medicine has added kundalini, meditation, and yoga to its clinical studies, as well as its roster for a possible element of a healthy life. These exercises, postures, expressive movements, meditation, breathing methods and concentration patterns do more than stretch the body. They have been proven to be a source of psychological growth as well as a source of physical health.

This corporeal energy is just the kind of doorway to something that exists inside our flesh and bone. We've been calling our body just that. A body. But a lot of the spiritual adepts call what we actually inhabit by three names.

The first name is the material body, corpus. This is the body that we all know and love that walks us through the day and slides between soft sheets at night.

The second name is the subtle body, anima.

The third name is spiritus, the Original Face or Spiritual Embryo. This is the embryo of Buddhahood.

All the yogic systems of the East talk about the subtle body. Eastern and Western practitioners of Chinese medicine or Western alternative sciences work from charts showing channels that carry life force and have focal points. Acupuncturists, for instance, work with the meridians of the body, opening channels that are blocked by stimulating certain points with hair-thin needles.

Subtle bodies and their charts figure into Chinese alchemy and classical Chinese medicine, but also found expression over the centuries in the Western esoteric investigations of Rosicrucianism, Theosophy, and the work of Rudolph Steiner, Gurdjieff and Max Heindel. Subtle bodies are spoken of in Western culture as far back as the Jewish Kabbalah. The subtle body does not show up in MRI scans. It hasn't been mapped out, although some recent investigators attempting to film emanating energy have developed Kirlian energy photographs. Similarly, spiritual energy described as auras has been categorized by color. However, neither express the essence of a subtle body.

The stuff of kundalini yoga can't be measured in ohms and other electrical measurements. Although it doubtless has expression in bio-chemical form, this is the essence of the spirit in its intersection with matter. Certainly energy, whether in caloric form or in bio-electric transmissions, is involved.

Awakening this coiled serpent at the bottom of your spine is not easy. Perhaps this is fortunate, as the results, unmonitored and controlled by experts, can be extreme. Like awakening a cobra too quickly, it can be wonderful but dangerous.

Nonetheless, using an observation-based version of the scientific method, we can conclude that many humans have had this experience, as it has been documented repeatedly.

So why would you want to awaken the kundalini?

Because, the energy called the kundalini is the juncture where the body meets the other elements of consciousness. Activation of the kundalini spreads this primal energy up along channels called nadis, through the centers of the chakras, with proper coaching. Occasionally pain is described, and certainly the sensation of heat, pleasure, even ecstasy is reported. Enlightenment, or spiritual awakening, is the ultimate result.

Preparation, however, is key. It has been said that a master in the tradition of the release of kundalini energy knows that the preparation for kundalini release is more important than the actual release itself.

Hatha Yoga is one proven method used for preparation of the body for release of the kundalini. These exercises of body posture and body breathing use dynamic energy, called prana, to prepare for the release of the latent energy of kundalini. When a student is judged by the teacher to be ready, the proper exercises are given to produce a kind of inner heat that will awaken the kundalini.

Meditation, visual imagery, even concentration can be used to help awaken the kundalini. Mantras (chants) or yantras (visual revelatory symbols of cosmic truths) are usually the prescribed methods.

Yogis who want to maximize the power of their prana, or energy, often practice the path of celibacy. They not only have to abstain from sex with others or even themselves, they have to train themselves not to even think about sex. A Chinese version of this would speak of qi and the preservation of jing for the purpose of awakening. The preservation of sexual energy allows it to be directed and used for heating the starting point of the body or activating the kundalini and the kundalini yoga chakra system, opening the chakras rather than it being lost in acts of pleasure or for making babies.

Certainly you have noticed sensations of energy and warmth in the nether regions involved with sexuality. Powerful hormones are released through activation of sexual energy. Dopamine, the hormone released through sexual attraction, lights up the brain. Oxytocin, released at orgasm and interestingly also during childbirth, results in bonding, rejuvenating a relationship and ensuring survival of the species.

In Buddhist traditions, the final practice for awakening kundalini, the starting point of the body, involves aspects of alchemy, the union of solar and lunar energies within the central channel. In Chinese classical medicine and alchemy, this is the yin and the yang, and has parallels in Western alchemy and other spiritual traditions. When the starting point is fully activated it appears as a Golden Embryo, the Original Face. It transforms you into a fully enlightened being.

KEY CONCEPTS
- Kundalini is a form of the Philosopher's Stone, a physiological activation of energy and consciousness evolution.
- Spiritual energy, or prana, travels through power centers called chakras in the body, from root to crown chakra, to awaken the kundalini.
- These chakra channels must be opened, methodically and carefully,often through inner yogas, which may include sexual yoga.
- This energy is dormant within each human body and represents super-consciousness when fully activated by opening the inner energy meridians.

57

CHAPTER NINE
Mysteries of the Void
The Super Powers of Zero

As we grow to understand the great union of opposites, the trikaya, and the rediscovery of the Original Face, we move closer to that moment when the Golden Embryo shines brightly just before disappearing into the void. What happens then at the moment of enlightenment? First, it is important to realize that the doorway to mind and spirit is within you. Our journey has shown us discoveries made in ancient times by humankind who used sacred techniques to return to the starting point of the body to recognize, realize and activate the trikaya — the union sometimes known as body, mind and spirit. Elsewhere it is more accurately called the "body," the "subtle body," and the "super-subtle body."

All bodies intersect at the starting point of the body. This is the beginning from which all else flows. As Archimedes, the ancient engineer who invented the fulcrum, put it so well, "Give me a place to stand and I can move the world." If Archimedes was going to move our consciousness into higher places, he would most likely select the starting point of the body.

But what exactly is the starting point of the body?

Seekers of truth have sought the answer to this question for millennia, and not just in the East. Champions and followers of Christendom have long sought the Holy Grail, the cup that Christ used for communion with his disciples during the last supper. He passed the cup of wine saying, "This is my blood, poured out for many, sealing the new agreement between God and man." Perhaps the quest made by the Crusaders and so many others for so long, to find the Holy Grail, symbolized the search for transformation of the body that we call enlightenment.

Western alchemists were on a similar quest for the Philosopher's Stone.

The Philosopher's Stone can easily be interpreted as the starting point of the body, and any deep examination of alchemy unearths the fact that Sir Isaac Newton spent far more time and brainpower on alchemical experiments than on inventing new forms of math and modern physics.

Although often referred to as the substance with which lead and other metals could be turned to gold, in fact, the Philosopher's Stone was a joining point between matter and spirit.

The search for this alchemical wedding, and transcendence, was of much interest to Carl Jung and formed the Western part of his investigations into human psychology — a study that also included examinations of Eastern practices, symbols and thought in an effort to create a synergy of understanding.

Buddhism played a role in developing the understanding of our bodies as doorways with access to perception and understanding, as well as joy, fulfillment and completion.

What lies at the very core of Buddhism? What vision of Golden Non-Duality did Siddhartha see under that Bodhi Tree when he became enlightened?

Perhaps it was his Original Face and the realization of the importance and experience of Nothingness, the Void. It is the experience of nothingness that is the ultimate goal spoken of by many great spiritual adepts.

There is a blank side to all experience. It is the opposite of vibration in our experience. The Chinese call the positive, male, earthy side that vibrates and is visible and tangible, "yang". The negative, female, spirit world of "yin" is the opposite of yang. There is a corresponding concept of one and zero. In the binary numerical system used by computers, combinations of one and zero are formed to create all possible numbers.

Think about it. You can imagine an infinite number of numerical sequences that have importance and meaning in your life: phone numbers, security codes, identification numbers, licenses and addresses. Some numbers guide us or determine locations, such as with longitude and latitude or GPS points. Other numbers define the health of your body as determined by your hematocrit number, blood pressure, cholesterol count, and heart rate. But there is one important number that stands out from all others. There is a center for all numbers, a starting point for numbers, just as there is a starting point for the body. For numbers, it is zero. And so perhaps it is for bodies and for ourselves.

The core of every religion or philosophy rotates around nothingness. The famous existentialist philosopher, Jean-Paul Sartre, analyzed the place of nothingness within consciousness to promote the idea of the basic freedom of man as an answer to the philosophies of determinism. In his book, *Being and Nothingness*, he wrote about the ability of consciousness, within the human body, to conceptualize possibilities and to make them appear, or to annihilate them.

Prince Siddhartha was raised in the Hindu tradition. His religion and culture had a particularly grim outlook on reality. Humans were said to live in *samsara*, a wheel of life full of suffering. After a life of suffering, even a reincarnation to another life would not relieve suffering. The degree of suffering could be greater or smaller, but it was still suffering. Siddhartha felt there had to be some other essential truths about existence that could be answered here and now.

He abandoned his life of luxury to focus on that quest. Siddhartha entered a life of asceticism and meditation. Finding all this wandering and seeking to be ultimately unsuccessful, he sat down for a very long time in purposeful meditation under a Bodhi tree, waiting to find the truth. What happened to him under that tree is the central focus of Buddhism. He achieved self-realization there at the age of thirty-five. He saw his Original Face, his true self, the pure being he was at the moment of conception – The Golden Embryo. He became the Buddha or Awakened One. For the next forty-five years, he taught his *dharma*, his insights, and died without much ceremony.

Central to the Buddha's dharma were the Four Noble Truths, which hinge around the problem of suffering or any dissatisfaction with life. He realized that desire or craving is what causes suffering. Attachments cause suffering. His Four Noble Truths are:

All beings inevitably encounter suffering *(duhka)*.
The cause of suffering is attachment to one's desires *(samudaya)*.
By letting go of attachments one can avoid suffering *(nordha)*.
To let go of attachments one must follow the path of the Buddha *(marga)*.

Once the Four Noble Truths are understood, the dharma goes on to describe an Eightfold Path toward dealing with desires and cravings, and a worthwhile path it is; one that works, in fact, within any other belief system.

The Noble Eightfold Path is as follows:

1. Right View
2. Right Intention
3. Right Speech
4. Right Action
5. Right Livelihood
6. Right Effort

7. Right Mindfulness

8. Right Concentration

It is believed that by following these eight instructions on life one can avoid or even transcend suffering and attain self liberation or Buddhahood.

So what Siddhartha was actually saying was that suffering cannot exist with zero attachments.

He was talking about "nothing."

No Buddhist would tell you that Siddhartha was sitting under the Bodhi tree thinking all this up. Thinking, after all, could be considered a form of desire, or even a servant of desire.

No, what Siddhartha did under the Bodhi tree was to *not* think. He opened himself to the void. He emptied himself to allow the truth in nothingness to find him within the consciousness that holds all possibilities.

Think about it. Not thinking is the goal of meditation. Not thinking is a goal of contemplation. But this not thinking is a very active not thinking. This is not thoughtlessness in a social or cultural context, but in a biological one.

Siddhartha was a person with a body and a secret power just like yours. He was able to use his body to achieve enlightenment. He came to understand, in a fundamental way, what the purpose of existence was. He found meaning and joy in that truth.

We have no way of scientifically measuring what Siddhartha experienced in his awakening. However, we can state that this awakening is something that happened in a body, and can be reproduced in any human body. Buddhists have practiced techniques to achieve spiritual awakening with remarkable effects. In meditation, if all the stages are properly completed by an individual, all that is becomes one.

Inside and out.

Past and future.

Present and matter.

One.

One becomes one—through nothingness —The Void.

Each defines the other.

A system of yoga can work with the body to activate this singularity, this connection resulting in superhuman powers.

Plenty of evidence has been gathered to show that Chinese inner alchemy, which is based on harnessing one's sexual energy to activate full brain consciousness, has good affects on human bodies.

We can see that we are a microcosm that reflects the macrocosm. We as individuals exist not in a vacuum, but in a social network connected to Nature.

What happened to Buddhism from the Buddha's enlightenment until now? Of course, like any great religion, there are long books dealing with those two and a half thousand years. Suffice it to say that now there exist more or less three versions of Buddhism, each of which differs significantly in its description of the path to enlightenment and liberation from suffering. Hinayana Buddhism is called the "lesser vehicle" because it is considered fundamentally self-centered and incomplete by the other branches, the Mahayana and Vajrayana traditions. The Vajrayana tradition claims to be the most complete form in that it contains all the practices of the other two branches including esoteric practices such as heat, dream and sexual yoga so powerful as to result in enlightenment in one lifetime.

Hinayana and Mahayana Buddhism were essentially associated with ascetic practices, which evolved into monastic university systems. The history of Buddhism is essentially a series of transitions. It is an outgrowth of single body experiences, solitary paths of yogis seeking spiritual liberation. These explorers elected to attempt to take the yogic systems they learned and perfected and created a university system to transmit knowledge.

Their knowledge brought the ability to use exercises and methods to awaken latent connections of the body to the subtle bodies, "full activation of the brain."

In any case, Hinayana and Mahayana are both rooted in the basic teachings of the Buddha, but stress different aspects of his teachings. While Hinayana seeks the liberation of the individual, the follower of the Mahayana seeks to attain enlightenment for the welfare of all beings. This attitude is embodied in the Mahayana ideal of the Bodhisattva, the spiritual warrior whose outstanding quality is compassion and helps others to achieve enlightenment.

And so, the central concept of the Void as experienced by the Buddha is an experience that is accessible to all. He saw a Golden Embryonic version of himself dissolve into nothingness. Nothingness, but with meaning. The Void, or *sunyata* in Sanskrit and *stong pa yid* in Tibetan, involves the interrelationship of things to the extent that nothing has an absolute identity.

The Sunni Sutra states that the famous attendant to the Buddha, Ananda asked, "It is said that the world is empty, lord. In what respect is it said that the world is empty?" The Buddha replied, "Insofar as it is empty of a self or of anything pertaining to self. Thus it is said, Ananda, that the world is empty."

Brenda Rawson, in her work, *The Tara Book,* written with Gehlek Rinpoche, points out that sky as a metaphor for the Void is commonly found in Tibetan art. The sky offers emptiness to the clouds as the Void is the space in which objects appear to us in our attachments and desires.

Nothingness is not the opposite of something, or even the absence of something. The two are connected like yin and yang. Somethingness arises out of nothingness. Like a giant blank slate, all possibilities can be drawn as all desires are visualized.

Another way to look at this concept of nothingness is to think of it as *potential* somethingness. It could also be thought of as the root of being. In Zen Buddhist teachings we find this idea of being coming from non-being. The Heart Sutra even states that "being is not different than non-being and non-being is not different from being." In truth they are both the same. It is only our differentiating consciousness that fools us into thinking this material world is any more "real." As quantum physics tells us, what we think of as a solid, material world is actually made up of infinitesimal bits of energy rather than matter, with immense areas of space within them.

From the experience of the Void comes, it is said, an astonishing truth. An individual, who has done his work with the body, loses his identity and discovers his true source of being, or consciousness. To experience true nothing, we experience the source of true meaning, true spirit.

In Chinese alchemy and qi gong this is called Attaining the Tao or Returning to the Source. In Zen practice it is called seeing your Original Face. This phrase comes from the famous Zen *koan* or spiritual riddle "What was the face you had before birth?" This is the completion stage of meditation, creating the Immortal Fetus, a Golden Embryonic version of the meditator.

Zen Buddhism, whose goal is the realization of the void through meditation and contemplation, is actually a Chinese form of Buddhism. Its basics are heavily influenced by the insights of Taoism. Methodologies and trappings may be different, but the goals are the same.

We can call this a Golden Singularity. It is the fusion of zero and one, pre-birth and post-birth spiritual energy. Let's just suppose now that this Golden Singularity is the same embryonic enlightenment (*tathagatagharba*) spoken of in Buddhism – the seed of Buddhahood in every human being.

This is the source of your own superpowers.

KEY CONCEPTS
- All bodies intersect at the starting point of the body.
- Our bodies contain doorways with access to perception and understanding as well as meaning, joy, fulfillment, and completion.
- Consciousness is the necessary friction point between being and nothingness.
- Letting go of attachments brings us to nothingness; through nothingness we become one. All becomes one.
- Although Buddhism was the first to state the importance of the Void, it exists implicitly at the heart of all spiritual disciplines.
- When you see your Original Face you see a Golden Embryonic version of yourself dissolve into nothingness.
- In China, shattering space or void is a description of the completion stage of meditation.
- The Golden Singularity is a fusion of zero and one, prebirth and postbirth spiritual energy, the seed of Buddhahood in every human body.

CHAPTER TEN
An Experiential Interlude of the Real Now

Your superpowers are available now. You are capable of attaining true consciousness, now!

Instant peace, instant understanding – you can experience all the joy and wealth of love and peace born in true spiritual leaders and true practitioners of spiritual paths.

It's such an overwhelming thought; one doesn't immediately consider it attainable.

But even now, as you read this text, you enjoy a glimpse of what we're talking about without fear of the jolt of kundalini, or the searing realization of trikaya.

No, just you, this book, and the universe.

William Wordsworth wrote a famous poem called *Intimations of Immortality* in which he related his feelings of connection to the spiritual in the natural world. And that's just what we're talking about here – intimations, glimpses.

Because the "you" reading these words has everything a Zen monk, or an alchemist or Buddha or Jesus Christ had for tools. You're exactly the same as them. Exactly. Nice to know this, right?

So, sit comfortably. Breathe deeply. No need for chants or yoga, at least for now, but you'll need an atmosphere without distractions. A little soft music you like won't hurt, and some soothing tea. You really can't be sick or hungry either.

There.

What do you do? Meditate?

Contemplation might be a more accurate word.

Now, consider.

Look out of your eyes. Hear what you are hearing. Taste what's in your mouth and smell whatever is in the air. Feel what's going on around you through the skin.

These are the avenues of sensory awareness provided by your body. And there you are at the intersection of this sensory awareness. But reach out with whatever is at that intersection. All your organs of perception can also separate you from your surroundings. If these modes of perception are muted or even tuned differently, different sensations happen.

Just feel this a bit, and contemplate.

Eventually you will become more aware of the fact that there's not as much between In Here and Out There as you thought.

You'll also start to notice your thoughts.

If you can, be an observer of your thoughts, not attached to them and not moved by them. You, after all, are not your thoughts. They rise up.

This is not the past.

This is not the future.

This is now.

Moreover, it is a remarkable now, in that it is the Real Now, the Eternal Now.

As you contemplate this, you may receive glimpses of what this Eternal Now really feels like. Whatever this stuff that we call consciousness is, it is loosened from its bonds of identity and goes deeper into infinity. You start to think of this consciousness as active. It is real. And you get a hint of a suggestion that says:

"There's something more than just a body here sparking off awareness that knows it's aware. It's a whole universe, a cosmos... maybe more... looking out at our hands, sipping warm tea."

This is the real me looking out at Real Reality.

In this state, an intense and calm awareness does not negate the body. The body is part of the dance. The body's interconnection with the air it breathes, the ground it sits upon, the sky above becomes obvious. Without distractions, one feels part of everything, and that feeling is wonderful.

This interconnectedness is often reported in nature. Wordsworth was moved to write about it often. Sometimes it's called Nature Mysticism but really that makes it sound a bit unreal. You may walk in the woods on a beautiful day, feeling good, and letting truth seep in. Pursued and nurtured, it's more intense and rewarding, but on a gentle, accessible level. And just about everyone has felt this kind of experience and knows that a key to relaxation and peace is to get away into Nature for a while.

That tickle of Reality can be pursued, though, on deeper levels. This feeling of oneness with the universe is just the start.

By learning the way to recreate the environment for this experience of walking in the woods as yoga, one can pursue it and deepen spiritual experiences on this level. Notice that "getting away from it all" means cutting off the clanking, complicated distractions of industrialized society, civilization and culture.

These kind of experiences, and deeper, were and are common amongst pre-industrialized societies. From them grew what may have been the roots of yoga and these exercises. We speak of it as shamanism. The shamanistic path was centered in nature.

The goal of a practical exploration of these issues is a personal thing. You can't build your upper body muscles by lying on the couch reading body builder magazines. You have to exercise. Push-ups help. Body building machines work well. But to go deeply into the discipline, people use free weights and trainers.

So for your rise to super powers, you merely have to use light meditation and contemplation, or even visualization, to get rewards, to see the truth, to glimpse some of the power.

You don't have to believe in spirit to feel the power of your spirituality.

You just need a different perspective.

No need to believe any of this. Just try on this point of view. Taste it and feel it.

Your body is a part of a system of the interplay of matter and energy, constructed of information.

Your mind is a part of another system of information, interconnected. A better word: the subtle body.

Spirit? Super-subtle body.

By obtaining this different perspective through established exercises, the Original Mind is reactivated. That part of us, the Observer who watches our thoughts and who feels these powerful truths, becomes the source of our being. This underlying deep stream of information becomes deeper and wiser with exercise.

Beyond higher consciousness comes the deep abiding sense of not just being part of this consciousness, but of purity, value, and truth. This can be called a Union with God, though not in a theistic way. Those who enter into the more extreme forms and choose to return and help others become our spiritual leaders. Spiritual teachings used to achieve spiritual goals last. However spiritual teachings used to further the goals of politics, society, and culture become dogmas, useful for the perpetuation of societies, but not always for spiritual quests.

This scientific method, in the form of thought experiments with the body was used by ancient cultures to devise methods and techniques to attain insight and perception of meaning.

Modern science has not yet developed the means to measure mind and spirit – the subtle body and the super-subtle bodies.

KEY CONCEPTS
- A state of true consciousness – an enlightened state – is possible at any moment of any individual's life.
- Meditation is a vital tool in removing the distractions that cover our perceptions of True Reality.
- True Consciousness – a profound understanding of True Reality – is key in understanding the path to inner and outer peace.
- The true origin of human consciousness is enlightenment.
- Fully mastering inner illumination represents true freedom and the discovery of ultimate meaning.

CHAPTER ELEVEN
Secrets Revealed
The Six Yogas of Naropa

The advanced techniques of the Six Yogas of Naropa accelerate the process of enlightenment. In fact, these methods include some of the most effective methods for achieving the union of the trikaya. These techniques may bring you experiences of enlightenment such as Prince Siddhartha had under the Bodhi Tree or perhaps even Jesus while in the wilderness. Techniques that were once held secret within ancient lineages are now much more available. Superpowers are possible to attain with the help of reputable trained masters and dedication and sincerity on your part.

What is unique about the Six Yogas of Naropa techniques is that they represent an ancient body of knowledge, methods, and techniques – from times before written history – which transform ordinary consciousness to enlightened consciousness. These techniques could enable you to transcend the normal barrier between the enlightened world and this world. While both are essentially the same worlds, we have to be initiated into esoteric perspectives and techniques to see for ourselves.

This collection shares in common the capacity to fully open the energy meridians of the body. These yogic practices all have the possibility of leading the practitioner to complete enlightenment. Different teachers have emphasized different practices, so collections vary depending on the teacher and location. Often a mahasiddha, a tantric shaman, would have a favorite technique that worked with great leaps of consciousness. Different mahasiddhas, enlightened lamas or yogis, went to different teachers who may have had a favorite technique. There will always be six in a collection, although comparing three different collections; you might see three slightly different variations. Some lineages have an extra technique and some have been lost. Some have extra techniques. Adding them up may give you eight different yoga techniques, but the collections themselves always have six.

There are also collections called The Six Yogas of Niguma, named after the female consort or sister of Naropa. Female mahasiddhas also had their collections of techniques and passed them down. These lineages embrace the divine feminine; the power of female energy is in the framework. But in all cases, these collections are similarly based around heat yoga, clear light yoga, and illusory body yoga. This is an ancient body of knowledge that emphasizes the development of qi through heat yoga, which allows the subtle body to function independently from the physical body.

These six yogas derive from original Indian shamanic and yogic methods of inner power development. The set was developed to harness the prana or qi of the human body to achieve full brain activation. Each of the techniques is considered a complete method of transcendence in and of itself. A meditator who successfully practices the Six Yogas achieves the union of the trikaya at the completion stage.

The Six Yogas were practiced in tantric Buddhism in Bengal around the time of Naropa's life, but aren't really Naropa's original ideas. Actually, Naropa was a famous student of these techniques. He studied under Tilopa in India in the tenth century. Tilopa had been born into a Brahmin family but left his comfortable home, taking on a monastic life and traveling throughout India receiving many teachings from gurus. After receiving a transmission in a vision during meditation, he continued to wander but from that point on as a teacher. He is considered the founder of the Kagyu lineage in Tibetan Buddhism and appointed his most successful student, Naropa, as his successor.

Naropa successfully completed difficult hardships to prove himself a worthy student to Tilopa. These tasks later became known as The Twelve Trials of Naropa. At one time, Naropa had to build stone houses and then pull them down. The trials were situations of challenge and pain, testing Naropa's loyalty and devotion.

Naropa's trials were not without precedent or antecedent. Paths to enlightenment are not necessarily easy, even when following the "watercourse way." The Tao, it would seem, often flows over rocks, rapids and spectacular falls. Spiritual teachers often tested their potential and current students with extremely harsh conditions, demands, tasks, and practices.

Jesus Christ never promised an easy road for his disciples either. He sent them out saying, "Don't take any money with you; don't even carry extra clothes and shoes or even a walking stick; for those you help should feed and care for you. I'm sending you out as sheep among wolves. You will be arrested and tried and whipped in the synagogues." These trials, like Naropa's, tested sincerity and were meant to eliminate dilettante practitioners with only superficial interest. Followers who did not have the mental fortitude or devotion to traverse a path to its end would fail the trials. Those students who successfully passed through these trials demonstrated the highest level of sincerity and devotion. To master the more advanced spiritual disciplines takes the focus and dedication seen in Olympic athlete gold medalists. These paths are for the fervent and dedicated.

Tilopa

As a Tantric mahasiddha, Tilopa developed the Mahamudra method,
a set of spiritual practices that greatly accelerated the process of attaining
enlightenment. Image: Elista Karma-Kagyu Centre, Krasnodar, Kalmuc Republik
(South of Russia).

Naropa's trials bore fruit. His Six Yogas, up until recently, were secret advanced teachings that are the foundation of many Buddhist lineages. Masters within each lineage often have multiple collections. Known as whisper techniques, teachers instructed students in whichever technique that would most empower each student to activate the energy that triggers the experience of seeing the Original Face.

Previously only the most gifted students, who had passed through arduous trials successfully in traditional training methods, were given the oral instructions for The Six Yogas. By placing restrictions when choosing students for the teachings, masters preserved the integrity of the lineage and the restrictions prevented inauthentic students from corrupting or impairing the transmissions of their truths and methodology. Students would start with commonly known ritual practices. If they showed dedication, loyalty and integrity, then the energy techniques were given in secret.

These practices were ritualized in a ceremony. There is an energy transmission given along with passing on a yoga technique. The student benefits from the merging of minds with the person who explains it and transmits it. This is missing from traditional modern seminars or class structures. In a group retreat or private session, the student is first empowered. Then the student must practice and refine it to master the technique. And, as in the past, a spiritual student might go to a master to learn a practice and it might not work. Then the student might go to another teacher and then it might work. A student who perseveres and continues to seek training would get a variety of techniques; some working differently from the others.

The 10th century Indian tantric master Tilopa, source of the lineage on the Six Yogas of Naropa and its deeper foundation, which is mahamudra, once said,

Mahamudra cannot be taught. But most intelligent Naropa, Since you have undergone rigorous austerity, With forbearance in suffering and with devotion to your Guru, Blessed One, take this secret instruction to heart.

Is space anywhere supported? Upon what does it rest? Like space, Mahamudra is dependent upon nothing; Relax and settle in the continuum of unalloyed purity, And, your bonds loosening, release is certain.

Gazing intently into the empty sky, vision ceases; Likewise, when mind gazes into mind itself, The train of discursive and conceptual thought ends, And supreme enlightenment is gained.[1]

These ancient lineages represent an unbroken chain of teacher and student, master and disciple, extending to the present. This system of secret techniques locked away for ages, is now open for access. The

1 *Masters of Mahamudra: Songs and Histories of the Eighty-Four Buddhist Siddhas* by Keith Dowman, Suny Series in Buddhist Studies.

names and the methods are known. For those who want to master the techniques, retreats led by teachers of the lineages can be found.

However, thanks to translations of many of the world's spiritual teachings and the spread by modern communication, including the Internet, anyone can access these secret techniques. Properly practiced, these precious teachings have the capacity to allow anyone to achieve the kind of realization great spiritual teachers speak of during this lifetime – or at least during the death experience.

Now that these methods are more readily available, you have the power to benefit. You are welcome in the world of the Six Yogas. You don't have to give up your entire life or go through tremendous trials to receive the teachings. Now you don't have to go to some cave in Tibet in the middle of winter. These valuable methods are attainable to students with the ability and determination to learn these methods who can recognize their value and master them. Anyone can use these, anywhere. However some kind of supervision from a master is generally vital.

Naropa

Naropa is one of the most prominent and authoritative Indian mahasiddhas and masters of mahamudra and tantra. He received the mahamudra and tantra lineage teachings from his guru Tilopa and transmitted them to his disciple, Marpa, the Great Translator of Tibet.

In fact, anyone doing qi gong or yoga could or should be using some version because it is essential to include inner yoga. You can access both inner and outer practices and you need both. The inner yoga, subtle body practices are as much or more important than physical body practices. All are based on generating greater levels of inner heat or inner power, generating more qi or prana. So here follows descriptions of these methods, to give you a better idea of what they comprise.

Beginning with the foundation of all these practices is *tummo*, or inner heat yoga. Successful practitioners of this sort of yoga are able to generate intense energy within their central spiritual channel, which causes their entire body to become warmer. There are a variety of methods used to heat qi. Heat yoga generally includes regulation of the breath, concentration on the navel center or in the lower abdomen, and visualization of sacred syllables. Some practitioners meditated in the middle of four fires under the blazing sun, holding their breath for as long as possible.

Imagine a celibate monk, conserving his sexual energy, in a long meditation. He creates a surge of inner heat, enjoying a sudden kundalini activation, which recreates conception and causes a golden embryonic version of himself to appear. The subtle body embraces that version which dissolves into the subtle body, which then jumps back into the physical body. The goal of alchemy is achieved and a golden immortal is created, like the Buddha statues portrayed in gold.

The power of heat yoga would allow a person to sit outside all night in freezing conditions without discomfort. In fact, people demonstrated their ability by generating enough heat to dry several wet sheets draped around their naked bodies while meditating, sitting in a snowfield at high elevations.

It is said that Milarepa, the most well known Tibetan to have completed the Six Yogas, spent all winter in the Himalayan Mountains in 1100 AD dressed only in a light cotton garment. His student, Gampopa, could go into trance state in lotus position, without a break, for three days. Seeing him as a worthy student, Milarepa taught him the technique of heat yoga, knowing the key to achieving enlightenment is internal heat activation.

Heat yoga is one of the oldest practices, dating back to shamanic hunter-gatherer cultures. As you can imagine, this ability greatly increased survival in cold climates, as well as having a consciousness-illuminating effect. Heat yoga also compensated for nutritional inadequacy in winter months. A person who mastered heat yoga could be expected to live much longer than other people and maintain a much higher level of health.

This is the lost knowledge of the human race: generating enough heat in the lower torso, or chakra, recreates conception. Qi rises toward the head.

The core practice, underlying many civilizations, is to create a golden blueprint of the self; what the Original Face really represents.

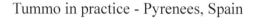

Tummo in practice - Pyrenees, Spain

Tummo, or "inner fire", is related to the description of intense sensations of body heat that are held to be a partial effect of the practice of Tummo-meditation, one of the Six Yogas of Naropa.

The next yoga is Clear Light Practice. In this yoga, forms of being dissolve into the void, encompassing all distinctions and boundaries. All differences are brought into one whole universal field of being.

Imagine, at the time of death, experiencing the radiance of a brilliant white light. In the *Tibetan Book of the Dead*, it is written that after you die there is an experience of luminosity that may be frightening. If you were to run from the light, it would prevent you from liberation and you would have a horrifying death experience.

In the Tibetan view, this white light underlies all realty. When a practitioner embraces and unites with the clear light of the void, liberation results. A person dissolves into clear light and is in union with the clear light. One experiences the light and comes out of it.

As one advanced practitioner related his experience, "I was lying in bed between sleeping and waking. I had a terrible feeling of being pulled into white light and not able to move. It was frightening and uncomfortable until I relaxed and went with it. Then I felt my whole being dissolve into white light, a luminosity, and then it felt wonderful. It felt like liquid white light. Then I came out of it and was back in my body."

The basic theory of this technique is that going into these altered states of consciousness represents complete dissolution of the body. Those altered states of consciousness are represented in this fundamental luminosity or clear light because the essence of the body is light. It is possible through the highest level of practice to refine the body back to the elemental structure of light. The practitioner totally unifies with a clear light luminosity that represents the emptiness of the void and higher knowledge.

Experiences of luminosity are common to many meditation practices. The Dalai Lama describes meditation as a means for the practitioner to achieve deeper and deeper levels of clear light during one lifetime. The founder of Zen Buddhism, Bodhidharma (China 470-543 A.D.) describes clear light experiences in his famous *Bloodstream Sermon.*

If, as in a dream, you see a light brighter than the sun, your remaining attachments will suddenly come to an end and the nature of reality will be revealed. Such an occurrence serves as the basis for enlightenment. But this is something only you know. You can't explain it to others. Or if, while you're walking, standing, sitting, or lying in a quiet grove, you see a light, regardless of whether it's bright or dim, don't tell others and don't focus on it. It's the light of your own nature.

Or if, while you're walking, standing, sitting, or lying in the stillness and darkness of night, everything appears as though in daylight, don't be startled. It's your own mind about to reveal itself.

The eternal lamp represents perfect awareness. Likening the illumination of awareness to that of a lamp, those who seek liberation see their body as the lamp, their mind as its wick, the addition of discipline as its oil, and the power of wisdom as its flame. By lighting this lamp of perfect awareness they dispel all darkness and delusion. And by passing this Dharma on to others they're able to use one lamp to light thousands of lamps. And because these lamps likewise light countless other lamps, their light lasts forever.

Long ago, there was a Buddha named Dipamkara, or lamplighter. This was the meaning of his name. But fools don't understand the metaphors of the Tathagata. Persisting in delusions and clinging to the tangible, they light lamps of everyday vegetable oil and think that by illuminating the interiors of buildings they're following the Buddha's teaching. How foolish! The light released by a Buddha from one curl between his brows can illuminate countless worlds. An oil lamp is no help. Or do you think otherwise? [2]

Clear Light Yoga involves a melting away of substance into the void, as being becomes nothing. That is, in this yoga forms melt into universal light. Thus, all distinctions and boundaries are dissolved.

Clear light experience occurs in the interface between waking and dreaming states. Basically, by working with this state of consciousness, one can tap into a luminous boundary, a powerful boundary, between mind and spirit. Clear light meditation harnesses this dreamlike awake state. Practitioners of this yogic method find themselves in a remarkably advanced state of consciousness. Clear light meditation involves the mind and body fully dissolving in the clear white luminosity of the void for extended periods of time between dreaming and waking. It is a profound and blissful experience of clarity.

The third of Naropa's Six Yogas is Dream Yoga. This yoga allows the practitioner to perform dream work even in his waking hours. This way the practitioner meditates when awake or asleep, and is able to step back from both experiences into a realization. Correct dreaming is a powerful tool in spiritual awakening. Once this realization is complete, the practitioner is taught to recognize when the body is asleep and the mind is dreaming.

This ancient practice was based on the idea that gaining lucidity or awareness that one is dreaming while one is dreaming provides a quantum leap of awareness. The practitioner uses self-suggestion until lucidity occurs and success is said to provide great spiritual and health

2 *Zen Teaching of Bodhidharma* translated by Red Pine, North Point Press, 1987.

benefits to the practitioner.

Dream yogic practices are transmitted by a master teacher, continuing his or her lineage, from master to student. Usually there is an initiation ceremony of some sort. True, every human being has the possibility of stumbling open moments of awakening. However, in the presence and under the tutelage of a person who is in a steady-state or continuum of this consciousness, you can expand upon these moments.

You may have noticed times when you accessed this ultimate field of pure thought, particularly in dreams and deep sleep when you dip into a vast well of consciousness. Most people though, are simply not aware this is happening. Dream states or deep trance states of consciousness are used toward achieving the trikaya, complete physical and subtle body union.

Realizing you are dreaming when you are dreaming is a Tibetan yoga practice. Dream yoga suggests that the more times you realize you are dreaming when you are dreaming the more potential you have to awaken both during your life and during the death experience. If you can maintain awareness during a dream experience you can maintain awareness during the death experience, which will enable you to achieve complete consciousness liberation, which is the goal of your existence, according to the esoteric tradition.

How does one achieve lucid dreaming?

During the day, keep on asking yourself, "Am I dreaming?" This sets up a pattern. Night dreams tend to be quite incongruous, as you realize when you try to describe a dream that defies reality. If you've established this pattern of questioning reality, kind of like pinching yourself all the time, in dreams you have the chance of repeating this "pinching" and asking yourself if this is the normal three-dimensional waking reality you're in.

There are many specific methods. One modern technique is to fall asleep with the strong intention to recognize the dream state as dreaming, while actually dreaming.

In hunter-gatherer cultures, dreams were used as guides. Dreams were survival tools to guide leaders to make decisions that would benefit all the people. Their shaman's interpretations of dreams were believed to be messages from guardian spirits, ancestors, or animal guides.

Dreams continue to guide men in these modern times. We have many examples of the power of dreams. Great scientists and inventors such as Isaac Newton, Albert Einstein, Niels Bohr, and Wolfgang Pauli were known to be great dreamers.

One night physicist Neils Bohr fell asleep after wrestling with the formulation of the structure of an atom. None of his ideas quite fit. As he slept, he dreamt of a solar system but instead of a sun with planets rotating around it, he saw a nucleus with electrons flying around it. Inspired by his dream, he tested this structural possibility and found it worked, winning a Nobel Prize for his findings.

Quantum physicist Wolfgang Pauli knew the power of dreams and often referred to his own as his secret laboratory. His dreams guided his scientific studies. During many dreams, he saw himself in discussion with other scientists about his projects. One night he dreamt he was speaking with Albert Einstein who urged him to accept a new dimension to reality, a psycho-spiritual dimension that fueled his concept for his ultimate life project, unified field theory.

German chemist Friedrich Kekule had changed his field of study from architecture to chemistry after becoming fascinated with the use of chemistry to solve crimes. He was studying the benzene molecule, when he fell asleep on a bus in London. His dream revealed the benzene molecule clearly formed in a ring shape, a serpent swallowing its tail, the most ancient symbol of alchemy.

Nobel prize winner Dr. Otto Loewi dedicated his life to finding a cure for tuberculosis. He was trying to learn how nerves transmit impulses, studying but not finding the answer. One night he fell asleep and had such a vivid dream that he grabbed paper and scribbled out some notes. In the morning, he looked at the notes and they made no sense at all. The next night he had another vivid dream that brought him understanding as to how nerve transmissions work. He discovered the secret of nerve impulses from not one, but two dreams.

Canadian Dr. Frederick Banting devoted his life to trying to find the cure for diabetes. His reason was personal; his mother had passed away from diabetes. There was a known link between insulin and diabetes, but not how it worked. Frustrated by his inability to discover the interactive process, he fell asleep one night while working on the problem. His dream explained the solution he was unable to find while awake. Experiments proved his dream correct and he was awarded a Nobel Prize in medicine for his work.

Inventor Elias Howe was working on an idea, a machine that would sew. He had worked on designs but hadn't found one that worked. One night, he fell asleep at his desk while working. He dreamt he was in

Africa, running from savage natives. They caught him and put him in a huge pot of water, lighting a fire beneath it. They were planning to boil and eat him. In his dream he kept trying to climb out of the pot. Each time the natives poked him back in the pot by pushing pointed spears at him. Repeatedly, he tried to escape the boiling water only to be met with the sharp end of a spear. Howe awoke, sweating and gasping in terror. He thought about his dream and realized that the spears each had a hole at the tip, like a very long needle. He realized he had the solution to his sewing machine design.

Inventor Thomas Edison believed in the power of dreams. He was known to sit in a chair with a metal ball in each hand while he fell asleep. When the ball dropped, he would awaken and write down ideas from his dreams. He used the concept that a state of consciousness that involves a brain shift or acceleration has capacity to result in great intuitive or scientific ideas. His intent helped; he was looking for solutions and inspiration.

Other dreams bring solutions without intentional dreaming, because a person's desire for a solution in a waking state continues over into the sleep state. Du Pont Corporation set up a high-speed machine to make Kevlar vests for American soldiers to wear during the Gulf War. Unfortunately, the machine had a tendency to break down. An engineer working on the problem dreamt that he was part of the machine. Water was spraying everywhere, over hoses and springs. After awakening, he realized the hoses were collapsing and that springs would keep them open. Improvements were made on the machine, preventing breakdowns and likely saving many soldiers' lives.

An important part of brain function is sleep and dreams. Historian Roger Ekirch, of the University of Virginia, described a time prior to the industrial revolution when people slept in two four hour segments, bridged by an interval of "quiet wakefulness." Often people would spend that interval contemplating, sharing, and discussing their dreams. Then people were less likely to have separate sleeping quarters, so it was natural to discuss dreams with fellow sleepers. Dreams were looked upon as messages from deceased relatives, as windows into the future, or as guidance from God.

Now, wakeful nights are more likely spent watching the clock or reading in bed between sleep periods. Electronic entertainment has replaced the novelty, inspiration, and pleasure of dreams, along with dream analysis and discussion of dreams. Chronic sleep deprivation is now more prevalent. A minimum amount of sleep is required to repair and heal the body. You need an excess of sleep to use the sleep state creatively.

You can recapture the mystery and inspiration of dreams by keeping your own dream journal. A notebook and pen under the bed, in a drawer, or on the floor nearby are all the tools you need. In dreams you may communicate with another probable self. You may tap into future possibilities in dreams. You can benefit from the creative process of dreaming. Write down every dream you remember. The potential to discover who you really are is possible within dreams. Synthesis occurs in sleep when the world of dreams and the outer reality of daily life are woven together. Bridging the gap is the key to your true spiritual path.

It is relatively normal to have a clear dream of an event only to find it come true in a month. Predicting the future – how does that happen? Think of the possibilities of a time slip where dreams occur outside of time and space and you have the capacity to access incredible information using the power of your dreamtimes.

On another note, combining hypnosis with dream suggestion and the placebo effect can have staggering healing capacity. Add Chinese medicine and qi gong and results can be incredible.

With dream yoga, the goal is actually to realize you are dreaming while you are dreaming. What you think is real is much closer to a dream than reality. The more you explore the dreamlike or mirage aspect of who you think you are and what you think is real, the more you disconnect the bonds that keep you from reaching the full potential of your enlightenment — who you really are at the deepest level.

Unlike the idea of dream analysis put forth by psychoanalysts like Sigmund Freud and his protégé Carl Jung, the Tibetan cultural interpretation of dreams is concerned less about content and meaning of dreams and more about the nature of dreaming itself. Dreams, what are they? They occur in REM sleep (Rapid Eye Movement) while your physical body rests and heals. But more, they underlie the secrets of your existence. In a lucid dream, one is aware that every person is a variation of the diversity of the underlying universal existence.

In dream practices, first you should know that dreams hold a secret potential for your spiritual journey. You may think that your dreams are not real as compared to the experience of your waking life. But your dream is real. It is as real as your waking life, while your waking life may be as unreal as your dreams. Tenzin Wangyal Rinpoche, in *The Tibetan Yogas of Dream and Sleep,* reminds us to understand "that dream yoga applies to all experience, to the dreams of the day as well as the dreams of the night."

In a lucid dream, you can practice duplicating yourself. This practice increases your ability to mentally manipulate reality while in a subtle body. A master practitioner can mentally manipulate physical reality the way dream reality can be manipulated mentally, because all reality is mental.

In Tibet, there is a belief that if a yogi is able to have eight clear, lucid dreams, realizing dreaming is occurring within the dream, liberation will assuredly occur during the yogi's actual death experience.

At the highest level, a combination of heat yoga and dream yoga uses energy cultivation to result in the control of dreams. In some cases, practitioners have been known to use dreaming at this level for consciousness projection, out of body experiences, to find greater knowledge.

Another Yoga of Naropa is Illusory Body Yoga. This yoga gives the practitioner the ability to create and emanate an energy or illusory body at will. An illusory body is a dreamlike representation of your physical body, which is recognized as illusory as well.

The subtle body can function for periods of time outside the physical body. It can travel beyond space and time. The subtle body can have a totally vivid waking experience in inner reality. This is more solid than a dream, where everything can shift. Spiritual growth is accelerated when the subtle body is trained to have spiritual experiences in spiritual realities.

The idea is to use the subtle body, by developing the subtle body to have an experience from within the subtle body, rather than the physical body. This practice gives you superpowers. You gain the ability to function within an energy body, rather than just a physical body. This happens after death when clearly the physical body is left behind. But during your lifetime, you can gain the ability to use your subtle body independently. Amazing spiritual experiences result.

A monk meditating in a cave may connect to a specific deity that relays powers with very real out-of-body experiences. The subtle or energy body has its own reality. It can function independently to access spiritual information or experience spiritual acts in its own inner reality, or in dreams, or even in parallel dimensions. This is one experience that can be achieved before reaching Buddhahood.

Also, if the subtle body is very strong, the physical body will take on properties of the subtle body. Special powers are possible. For instance, one could appear or disappear at will. The energy body could so overlay the physical, that the person casts no shadow. An advanced practitioner could ascend to heaven in daylight. According to these traditions, a person can dissolve into pure energy.

In a classic Taoist story, three monks visited an emperor's court. The emperor wanted to test their spiritual and magical skills, so asked them to bring him peaches from a tree a thousand miles away. The three monks sat in meditation. One monk projected himself mentally to gather peaches. He was the first to arrive in the orchard and picked a lovely peach, but was unable to bring it back because he was not in a physical body. One sent a double of his physical body riding on his magical donkey. He arrived in the orchard, dismounted, and selected a beautiful peach for the emperor. However, the peach was lost when he mounted his spirit animal. One went in his spirit body, his subtle body. He saw the others in the orchard as well. But he was the only one who brought back a peach. To travel to other dimensions in a subtle body is possible. A subtle body is not limited by matter because the rules are different. A subtle body can transcend normal limitations of space and time. So traveling to the future or past would be normal, with interesting benefits such as meeting a teacher from the past.

The goal is to realize that the physical body is an insubstantial form projected by the subtle body. Illusory body yoga may allow a practitioner to travel to non-physical realms to access information.

There is another recent story of a Tibetan lama. He fell asleep one night and dreamed of a goddess or dakini. In the dream, she had an important lesson to give him. She wrote it down on a scroll of yellow paper and pressed it into his hand. When the lama awoke, he found a little rolled up paper in his hand.

What is important to know is that the practices associated with mahamudra draw upon instructions from multiple levels of Buddhism, to provide a range of approaches to enlightenment suited to the needs of various practitioners. Mahamudra is believed to enable one to realize the mindstream's innate purity, clarity and perfection, summed up by the term "Buddha Nature."

For a beginning experience, you might visualize yourself as who you really are, the deity deep within yourself. After a while, the recognition of the illusory nature of the human experience is realized. One perceives one's body as composed from the most subtle energy. It is what it truly is: a body of light, truly a Rainbow Body.

And another Yoga of Naropa is Mirror Yoga. This technique also reaffirms the illusory nature of the body. Your body is as real as a dream, as fragile as a soap bubble.

When you look in a mirror, you see yourself as an illusion. Biologists define a super intelligent being as any animal that recognizes itself in a mirror. So right away you can be assured that you are super intelligent!

Practitioners can get to the point of being in the mirror looking back at their physical body. Indeed, Mirror Yoga is a means for the subtle body to separate from the physical body.

Mirror yoga practice allows your consciousness to recognize that you are in more than one place at the same time. Just as in the subtle body activation that occurs in lucid dreaming, you are aware of being in two places or dimensions at the same time. Then, at the time of enlightenment you are in three places at the same time, in the subtle body embracing the Original Face while in the physical body.

This technique reminds you of how you exist in inner and outer dimensions of reality simultaneously. When you realize that your Original Face, which dissolves into emptiness, is the real you, then you see yourself dissolve into emptiness. So, you are actually emptiness.

Mirror yoga is similar to seeing your reflection of yourself in a mirror. You, as a physical body, are a reflection of the real you, which is the reality body, the Original Face. The most subtle body that dissolves is the real you; the physical body is not your real body. This reverses the normal conception, which is considered an illusion. You are less substantial the more you go from space to light to sound to matter. The most subtle body is the most refined, the most highly developed. The physical body is the one that is not as real.

In meditation, the ideal is to refine the mind-body energy to the level where you see your Original Face in an inner mirror experience. The mirror is essentially a doorway to your true self, representing the knowledge of who you really are.

When you meditate while looking in a mirror, you can experience the projection of consciousness. The mirror represents seeing the true you, your Original Face. Your reflection in the mirror is a metaphor for you being a reflection of the real you. Your body is the more dreamlike and unsubstantial, like a reflection.

You may try a concentration exercise by putting a candle in front of a mirror and meditating on the candle. You might meditate on your own image and change it visually. Or you may want to contemplate the following story.

Long ago, in China, a wise old monk placed a white candle next to a golden statue of Buddha in a room filled with mirrors. He then brought in the empress to show her the holographic, multidimensional nature of reality.

This story brings to mind the legend of the Web of Indra. At every junction in the net a vibrant, beautiful gem is nestled, each one reflecting all the other jewels contained in each junction of the net. The reflection of the jewels does the same thing as the point in a hologram. Every point of a hologram contains information regarding all other points. The jewels in Indra's Net similarly contained the whole thing. In the Web of Indra when any jewel is touched, all the other jewels are affected. It represents the hidden interconnectedness and interdependency of all things in the universe. So what you do to another person reflects on yourself. How you treat yourself reflects on the universe. There is no real inherent self.

Indra's Net challenges the notion of a solid, measurable universe. One jewel has the capacity to reflect the light of another jewel on the opposite edge of infinity. All that is seen is in reality a reflection of something else. There is no beginning or end. The transcendent wisdom at the core of our existence shines forth in the reflection of all light throughout the entire universe. The fact that all parts are simply a reflection of all other parts implies the illusory nature of all appearances. Therefore, appearances are not reality but a reflection of reality.

The capacity to reflect all things attests to the mind being a mirror of reality,which is projected from an underlying unified field.

Stephen Mitchell, in his book *The Enlightened Mind*, wrote:

The Net of Indra is a profound and subtle metaphor for the structure of reality. Imagine a vast net; at each crossing point there is a jewel; each jewel is perfectly clear and reflects all the other jewels in the net, the way two mirrors placed opposite each other will reflect an image ad infinitum. The jewel in this metaphor stands for an individual being, or an individual consciousness, or a cell or an atom. Every jewel is intimately connected with all other jewels in the universe, and a change in one jewel means a change, however slight, in every other jewel.[3]

Modern physicists find this ancient metaphor a useful and accurate description of the universe as well.

Indra's Net

Imagine a multidimensional spider's web in the early morning covered with dew drops. And every dew drop contains the reflection of all the other dew drops. And, in each reflected dew drop, the reflections of all the other dew drops in that reflection. And so ad infinitum. That is the Buddhist conception of the universe in an image.
Alan Watts [4]

As you picture the holographic examples, know this: when you see your Original Face dissolve into emptiness at the time of enlightenment, it is like a holographic experience. The whole universe is within you. Zen Buddhists call it "swallowing the entire ocean in one gulp." The smallest part contains the whole. So when you achieve Buddhahood, everything appears geometrically equivalent. All is united—material, subtle body, and super-subtle body. This single whole transcends birth, death, space, and time.

3 *The Enlightened Mind* by Steven Mitchell, Harper Collins, 1991.

4 Alan Watts Podcast - Following the Middle Way #3 alanwattspodcast.com.

When you contemplate your image in a mirror, your focus is on the insubstantial nature of our everyday experience. Mirror practice allows one's mind to open, to ventilate the solidity we typically attribute to our world, and especially to our "selves." It is an effective way of perceiving the dreamlike nature of reality and especially the true nature of "self", which is void.

These first five Yogas of Naropa may bestow Buddhahood on the practitioner quickly. However, they don't always work. So there is a sixth Yoga, Bardo, that ensures enlightenment at the time of death. Again, you need an experienced teacher to learn these techniques correctly.

Bardo, the Yoga of Death, permits the practitioner to determine their after-death destiny, including decisions about rebirth. Tibetan yoga emphasizes practices that allow the practitioner to prepare himself in order to overcome the fear of death. If the opportunity is missed to join with the radiant white light after death, a nightmarish result may follow. There could even be an unfortunate rebirth.

In the Tibetan framework, all these training methods are meant to assist in the death experience. The Bardo, after death, is most important because the majority of yogis don't achieve enlightenment while alive. So if you aren't successful in this lifetime, the opportunity is there at the end of life. If you are able to control your fear, you can use the death experience to achieve ultimate freedom, enlightenment. If you don't control your fear, you may go through the death experience with horrific visions and be reborn with all your memory wiped out.

All you have at the moment of death is the level of your present awareness as well as the depth of your meditation and spiritual practice. If you have practiced some of these successfully, you will be more capable of traversing the death experience with the goal of achieving enlightenment during and through the death experience.

The goal is to consciously dissolve the immortal drop into emptiness, the return to the void. As the physical body drops away, there is a gap of perception, which if consciously observed, results in the union of the subtle bodies. Using the techniques learned from dream yoga, one can consciously observe the process of dying without fear and distorted perception.

As death approaches, earth, water, fire and wind – the four elements of the body – begin to dissolve. They are no longer able to support consciousness. With each loss, the dying person undergoes a different sensation. At the end, the sense consciousnesses have ceased to operate. Conceptual consciousness dissolves. The winds withdraw from the right and left channels of the upper body and gather at the crown of the head and then descend to the heart and a pure white light is perceived. Winds from the lower part of the body then enter the central channel at the base of the spine and rise to the heart area. A red color appears. The white of the father's semen and the red of the mother's ovum unite at this most subtle form of consciousness called the Mind of Clear Light. Winds converge, bringing an appearance of thick darkness, and the dying person loses consciousness.

The Six Yogas of Naropa are effective methods to understand the true nature of Reality, using the physical body. Over the thousand years of their existence, many practitioners have realized fabulous spiritual truths and returned to tell the tale. It is their incredible power that enables you to read this now. This is the power of who you really are.

One can only hope that someday these Yogas will be practiced in the West with the fervency that hatha yoga is now, and with more comprehension of their true purpose.

Ati Yoga, also known as Great Perfection or Dzogchen, is the lineage connected to the Rainbow Body and uses space, light or darkness to unite these mother and child lights that bring us back to who we really are. When the subtle body and supersubtle body unite, the result is complete awakening. This is the ultimate superconsciousness, the you that lives at the end of the future before the beginning of the past.

Enlightenment or being "one with the Tao" or perhaps even "salvation" is the stripping away of the distractions of wants, desires, ego and personality, allowing the Real Self to come through. Enlightenment is a prioritization and comprehension of the nature of these things.

At first a yogi feels his mind is tumbling like a waterfall;
In mid-course, like the Ganges, it flows on slow and gentle;
In the end, it is a great vast ocean,
Where the lights of Child and Mother merge into one.
    Tilopa [5]

Your own life experience is an experience of the evolution of consciousness. You have the capacity to radically accelerate that evolution. Anyone reading this book could be the next Tilopa or Naropa. This

5 *The Song of Mahamudra,* trans. by Jack Kornfield, Shambhala, 1993.

could be you if you learn from a master, learn correctly, and practice methodically. Practice refines the body to a higher form. Perhaps you can achieve that body of light that appears translucent and leaves no shadow. Just as not everyone trains to climb Mount Everest, it is possible but takes dedication. In this case, it is the dedication to achieve a mind-body union that links inner and outer realities and enables the mind to recognize the source of itself, which is the fully activated starting point of the body, or Original Face.

This is the meditation theory of self-evolution and self-realization that underlies Chinese, Indian, and Tibetan cultures. Even now, Western science has begun to accept, study and become aware of the realities of these theories. When clearly understood, one is enabled to achieve enlightenment. The future of modern science lies in fully understanding this framework.

And it is available to everyone.

KEY CONCEPTS
- Spiritual masters have created systems or disciplines and practices to accelerate enlightenment safely for the benefit of the individual, society and the universe.
- The Six Yogas of Naropa are a collection of sophisticated practices developed to accelerate the realization of enlightenment.
- Thanks to better translations, the information on the proper practice of these yogas is now available, but supervision for these practices is recommended.
- The primary purpose of yoga is spiritual enlightenment.
- Heat yoga is the basis of spiritual illumination and occurs in shamanic cultures as well.

CHAPTER TWELVE
Shamanism

The key in all these systems – whether Chinese, Tibetan or Indian – is to generate enough inner heat to transform the starting point of the body into the golden Original Face of non-duality and fuse it with the subtle body. Of course other cultures have used this same practice of generating inner heat including the Kung, a former gathering and hunting society living in the Kalahari Desert of southern Africa.

Those who have learned to heal are said to "possess" num. They are called *num kausi*, "masters, or owners, of num." Num resides in the pit of the stomach and the base of the spine. As healers continue their energetic dancing, becoming warm and sweating profusely, the num in them heats up and becomes a vapor. It rises up the spine to a point approximately at the base of the skull, at which time kia results. Kinachau, an old healer, talks about the kia experience: "You dance, dance, dance, dance. Then num lifts you up in the belly and lifts you in your back, and you start to shiver. Num makes you tremble; it's hot." Kia is "that altered state of the consciousness which is the key to healing." Num is "the Kung spiritual energy." Richard Katz [6]

Long, long ago, something started the lineage of awakened consciousness in humanity. It was shamanism, an ancient tribal system. The shaman, the spiritual leader of the tribe, could enter an altered state of consciousness at will. In this other reality, they journeyed to other realms to gain knowledge and power. The highly respected shaman then used this knowledge and power to help members of the community. Religion, medicine, philosophy and science evolved from these practices that worked with body, mind, and spirit. Shamanism is the ultimate historical source for all that we are talking about.

Knowledge was passed down through ritual and practice in the oral tradition prior to written history. Great thinkers like Socrates didn't write. Prince Siddhartha didn't pass on teachings by writing a book. Jesus Christ didn't write a book. Fortunately, historians did. We can thank the scribes who wrote down oral traditions for the *Bible*, the *Bhagavad Gita (Song of God)*, the *Tibetan Book of the Dead* and the *Dead Sea Scrolls*.

6 *Boiling Energy* by Richard Katz, The President and Fellows of Harvard College 1982.

Lama Surrounded by Mahasiddhas

Tibet, Eighteenth Century

The Sorcerer of Les Trois Frères, in a French Pyrenees cave, is an anthropozoomorphic figure with stag antlers and ears, owl eyes, a beard, bear or lion paws, a horse like- or fox like tail, and human feet. Anthropozoomorphic figures may depict shamans in ritual attire or spirit beings who guide the shamans.

You've just learned about the secrets of the Six Yogas of Naropa.

Essentially, the Yogas of Naropa are a combination of tantric and shamanic techniques. Working with the body, shamans connected with something beyond the body.

The shamanic path contains the original medical traditions of a people. Shamans themselves were leaders and often warriors or philosopher-kings. They worked with dreams and other methods of divination. Healing shamans used both physical and spiritual methods for working with the body.

Mircea Eliade, the great shamanic scholar, wrote that the shamanic traveler commanded techniques of ecstasy. The soul, or subtle body, was freed to roam at a distance. Through an experience of ecstasy, a shaman would travel roads in extraterrestrial regions with a guardian spirit to guide and protect through the dangers of a mystical geography.

Shamans brought to light the subconscious realm in the context of the challenge of labyrinths or overcoming demons. Rituals and ceremonies were not meant to be an end on their own but a visual structuring of an event to make it accessible. A vision taps into a great deal of spiritual power and truth. A fundamentalist, for instance, takes the reality of a literal translation and uses it as a vehicle for witnessing, a personal experience. There is a personal experience of Christ, or Allah, or Mary, or Shiva. There is a vivid experience of a subtle state reality. A belief that opens up a direct experience grows stronger.

A teaching shaman uses their personal experience for the good of others. The spiritual warrior, the Bodhisattva, takes the experience of enlightenment or spiritual awakening and makes a commitment to share the highest state of being for the good of fellow human beings. A Bodhisattva desires universal liberation and focuses on alleviating problems on a wider level by teaching others. A Bodhisattva has a vast open heart, called Bodhichitta, which inspires the Bodhisattva to bring happiness to all sentient beings.

But there are not only teaching shamans. There are also healing shamans. In India, the enlightened shaman was called a Mahasiddha. Essentially these were wonderful yogis who had great psychic and spiritual powers because of their advanced realization of inner powers.

If truth and enlightenment are achieved through the trikaya – through this joining of the body, the subtle body and the super-subtle body – and if the Philosopher's Stone is indeed the starting point of the body, that body has to be a healthy body.

The healing shaman represents the traditions for longevity medicines, for curing ills, and for creating the foundation of a healthy body. By sourcing traditions of spirit and nature and by knowing what herbs or roots to use, as well as when and how, the shaman uses elements of the spiritual to breathe energy and health into the body.

But also, in many traditions, there is a projection of the baser and misguided elements of human understanding. These are the bewitching shamans. They represent power through coercion, deception and illusion. Bewitching shamans parasitically prey on weaker beings. They are believed to be guided by malevolent deceased ancestors in many cases.

Fortunately there is also the tantric shaman, who was believed to have all the powers attributed to the other sorts of shamans, with the goal of full realization of nirvana. These shamans became mahasiddhas, those who had united the three bodies. Uniting the three bodies is the highest level of power.

In many of the ancient Asian civilizations, the first king or ruler was a tantric shaman. In China, these might have included the Yellow

Emperor and Lao Tzu, in a loosely mythic way.

These tantric shamans practiced physical male and female alchemy, but for spiritual purposes. They used dreams, visions and inter-dimensional travel in order to retrieve useful information from other realms for all the members of the tribe, clan or community. The Asian shamans also translated the inner meanings of dreams for the benefit of the tribe.

Like in other pre-industrial societies, the shamans in the East were believed to serve as intermediaries between the worlds of the living and the dead. They had the ability to guide the souls of the departed to their next destinations, which is similar to the Tibetan practice of P'howa, or transference of consciousness. This is a meditation practice that, applied at the moment of death, allows the practitioner to transfer consciousness through the top of the head to a destination of choice. Some lineages include this practice in their collection of the Six Yogas of Naropa.

In the small amount of available shamanic literature, the majority of descriptions of ascending or descending journeys to an upper, middle or lower world, are based on shamanic intervention on behalf of a student or patient. A shaman's journey is the defining practice of shamanic visionary experience.

Here's an interesting example of the relatedness of shamanic practices where there is no known historical connection. In some tribes of Siberia, far from Tibet, a proper shaman has to have experienced eight dismemberments of the subtle body. This experience is one of the key characteristics of shamanic initiation in what is now Russia.

This rite of dismemberment is also the basis of the Chod (cutting through the ego) practice of Tibetan Buddhism, where a practitioner visualizes dismembering themselves and offers body parts to various "guests" at a ritual feast.

This symbolic rite is obviously similar to the Christian Holy Communion. At the Last Supper, Jesus broke a piece of bread and shared it with his disciples. He said, "This is my body, given to you. Eat it in remembrance of me." This was not so much the sharing of the body, but as a metaphor for the interconnectedness of many bodies with one teacher.

One of the most remarkable aspects of ancient shamanism is its view that there exists, not just our world, but many worlds. Of course, for centuries humankind has fantasized about trips to the Moon or Mars or other planets throughout the galaxies. But the literature of science fiction has also described parallel worlds and different dimensions. Today, physicists speculate on this plausibility.

Multiple worlds have been the basis of the shamanic worldview for thousands of years or more. The Western physicists' rediscovery of the Buddhist Billion World Theory, in which the universe is seen as a multiverse containing worlds within worlds, has confirmed the essential shamanic worldview. According to modern string theory, the universe exists in multiple dimensions, side by side and within each other. We humans also live parallel lives in each of these dimensions. To wit: there are many parallel dimensions and our waking reality obscures our perception of these other worlds.

They are always present, but most of us cannot observe or visit them. Shamans say they can.

The pre-eminently shamanic technique is the passage from one cosmic region to another — from earth to sky, or from earth to the underworld. The shaman knows the mystery of the breakthrough in plane. This communication among the cosmic zones is made possible by the very structure of the universe.

Mircea Eliade [7]

Chinese shamans traveled the cosmos for centuries before the birth of organized religions. The most famous of all Chinese soul flights is described in the classic poem, *The Far-off Journey*, from *Chuchi* or *Songs of Chu*, dating to the third century BCE. The author described how he toured the universe:

Up to the Cracks of Heaven
Down to the Great Abyss
Going beyond non-action, I reach the Clarity.
Become a neighbor of the Great Beginning.
Dr. Roger Walsh [8]

There are different types of shamanism all over the world, from the Inuit Tribes in the North to the aboriginal Dreamtime in Australia.

[7] *Shamanism: Archaic Techniques of Ecstasy* by Mircia Eliade, The Bollingen Foundation, 1964.
[8] *The World of Shamanism: New Views of an Ancient Tradition by* Dr. Roger Walsh, Llewellyn Publications, 2007.

Shamanism might be said to be the source of all religion. Ultimately the spiritual insights and mental activities of shamanism are reflected by science in our particular fabric of reality, and here particularly in this examination of body, mind and soul and the trikaya.

The most famous shamans of ancient Chinese legend were the Eight Immortals. They symbolize happiness, prosperity and longevity. Some Chinese martial art techniques and qi gong practices are named after them. The Eight Immortals are said to be the gods who punish evildoers and encourage people to do good, help those in distress, and aid those in peril. They each came to immortality in different ways and each symbolizes different superpowers.

The Eight Immortals of Chinese Mythology

The Eight Immortals crossing the sea, from Myths and Legends of China, 1922 by E. T. C. Werner.
Clockwise in the boat starting from the stern: He Xiangu, Han Xiang Zi, Lan Caihe, Li Tieguai, Lu Dongbin, Zhongli Quan, Cao Guojiu and outside the boat is Zhang Guo Lao. Each immortal had a specific power that could be used to give life or destroy evil.

96

Zhang Guo Lao is represented as an old man riding a donkey, carrying a bamboo tube-drum with iron sticks. The tubes contained wands or phoenix feathers, which he used to forecast the future. According to legend, at the end of his journey he could fold up his donkey like a piece of paper and store him in his wallet. Then, when he wanted to travel, he would sprinkle water on his wallet and the donkey would reappear. He was given the magic art of prolonging life and was adept at holding his breath for extremely long periods of time. He was a master in the arts of alchemy and qi gong and was a healer, using herbal infusions. After death, his coffin was opened and found to be empty. Another example of the Rainbow Body? He is believed to guide those who have died to reincarnate into favorable realms and can give prophetic dreams. He is the patron deity for elderly men.

Zhongli Quan carries a fan and sometimes a peach and is considered leader of the Immortals. It is said that, having escaped from a lair of tigers and wolves, he turned to questions of immortality. He met with an old sage and received knowledge of the degree of heat necessary to produce the Philosopher's Stone and the Green Dragon method of swordplay. His magical palm leaf fan can revive and reincarnate the souls of the recently departed. He represents the military man.

Lu Dongbin wears a magic sword on his back, used to slay evil spirits and demons. In his hand he carries a flywhisk. He is said to have traveled the earth for over 400 years slaying evil spirits. He was very quick at learning at a young age and astounded his family with his ability to memorize thousands of lines. He wears the clothing of a scholar and is thought of as such. While wandering, he acquired supernatural invisibility by the Magic Sword technique from a Taoist adept. His pure yang sword makes him invisible to evil spirits and allows him to hide in the heavens as well as subduing the evil spirits. Having successfully endured ten ordeals, he was given a piece of the Philosopher's Stone, thus gaining immortality. His three-part beard symbolizes the three highest meditative levels. He is also the patron deity of barbers, magicians and jugglers.

Han Xiang Zi is the Happy Immortal who plays a flute made of purple bamboo that glows purple light in the dark. It is said that Han Xiang Zi could make flowers bloom by his will alone, and wild animals were soothed by his music. His flute plays the six healing sounds and can cause growth. He was given the secret for returning to a condition in harmony with nature. He is an expert on the mysteries of heaven and a master of the Five Phases of Energy. The sacred knots on his robe symbolize his ability to combine the two opposite energies – yin and yang—into the one original energy. Said to have fallen from a peach tree to his death, he achieved immortality at the moment of death. He is the patron deity of musicians

He Xiang Gu is the female immortal who carries a magical Lotus Flower along with healing fruits and herbs in her flower basket. Her flower can cultivate people through meditation and symbolizes her purity and the power of divine brilliance. Immortal Lu Dongbin rescued her from a demon with his magic sword. She was visited by a divine personage while a teenager and instructed to eat a powder of mica. This transformed her into an etherealized person with immunity from death. She was also given a magic peach and later gave up eating ordinary food. She helps the desperate needing divine intervention as well as marriage and family well-being.

Lan Cai is of questionable gender, sometimes seen as a woman, sometimes as a young boy, sometimes as an old man. She is a strolling singer, always shown wearing a tattered blue gown and only one shoe, carrying a basket, at the end of a long hoe, containing 108 flowers, plants, and branches from trees associated with Taoist arts of longevity, such as the chrysanthemum, peach blossom, pine and bamboo. In the winter, she sleeps in the snow while steam-like vapors rise around her, reminiscent of Tibetan heat yoga (tummo) practice. She is the patron deity of florists and brings joyfulness and attracts beautiful people. Her basket of flowers allows her to communicate with the gods.

Li Tieguai is depicted as a crippled beggar carrying a double gourd. It was told that his spirit would frequently leave his body to wander the land and heavens. One day his body was found and thought to be dead so was burned, as cremation was the custom. When he returned from his journey to find his body gone, he entered the first body he found, that of a lame beggar who had died of starvation. "Iron-crutch Li", always carries a crutch and a magical gourd, symbolic of universal medicine. He is a master of the Five Phases of Energy and able to manifest medicines and potions from his gourd. His gourd is often depicted with spiraling mist representing his soul and with a ball representing the Philosopher's Stone. It was said he would make himself small enough to sleep inside his gourd at night. He is the patron saint of the sick and injured.

Cao Guojui is always shown wearing formal court dress and carrying castanets or a jade tablet that gives him admission to court. Indeed, he may have been connected with the Sung Imperial family. It is said he was disgusted with the murderous behavior of his younger brother so left his wealth and royal position to go to a mountain retreat where he spent his days in spiritual study. He was visited by Immortals Lu Dongbin and Zhongli Quan, who instructed him in the secrets of perfection. He quickly mastered the techniques and became immortal himself. His magical castanets were played in a soothing and relaxing rhythm to encourage meditation and to assist his journey through the universe. His jade tablet also had the power to purify the environment. He is the patron deity of actors.

All of these Immortals began as ordinary men or women. They were combinations of doctor, alchemist, shaman, yogi, and exorcist. They used their power in virtuous pursuits and drove out demons, dark intrusions of matter that caused illness. They were linked to the world of enlightenment while still in a human body. Discovering their true self, they were able to attain their ultimate potential. Their techniques were ancient practices reminiscent of those used today. Indeed, many lineages found in martial arts and qi gong descended from these Immortals.

Their intent, when using super powers, was centered on virtue. Not surprisingly, in military shamanism, virtues of chivalry such as truth, honor, perceptiveness, and generosity of spirit are key components. Out of what historians sometimes call times of barbarism, arose qualities that are present in the ideal of fully evolved human beings.

The goal of helping those in need and teaching techniques for immortality, as seen in the schools of martial arts and the lineages of qi gong practices, is central to the ideal of the spiritual warrior, the Bodhisattva.

The Immortals demonstrate the powers derived from the amazing world of inner alchemy. The practices known to them have been passed down through the ages from master to student. The super powers of the Immortals are available to you through the current masters of inner alchemy and qi gong.

KEY CONCEPTS
- Underlying all spiritual, psychological systems, and medical systems is shamanism.
- The shaman has the ability to communicate with spirits and travel to other dimensions, being able to enter alternate realities at will.
- The conscious use of dreams has its most ancient origin in shamanism.

CHAPTER THIRTEEN
Patterns, Energy and the Flow in the Universe

Essentially all the systems from ancient Chinese sources – acupuncture, tai chi, traditional Chinese medicine, kung fu (*gong fu*), and qi gong – are based on the concept of an internal spirit-somatic energy called qi (chi). Like prana in Indian chakra work, qi flows along channels throughout the body. Good health and longevity for the human body may be primary goals of qi work, but that is just on the surface level.

What is this mysterious internal force? The father of Taoism, Lao Tzu, attempted to explain it:

> There is something formed in chaos,
> coming before heaven and earth,
> existing in the silent and tranquil void,
> it stands alone and unchanging,
> it pervades everywhere without becoming exhausted,
> it is the mother of heaven and earth.
> I do not know its name
> and so call it "Tao."
>   Chapter 25

The Seal of Lao-tzu

The Venerable Lao Tzu authored the *Tao Te Ching* (*Dao De Jing*), describing the Tao, and so is considered a legendary founder of the Taoist path. This is a way of transcending death by using the existing energy within the human body and following a way of life that stays true to the Tao.

In order to understand qi properly, an understanding of Tao is essential. Lao Tzu said that the attempt to put Tao into words is futile. It must be experienced, not merely studied. The experience begins from the starting point of the body and extends outward and upward to mind and spirit.

It cannot be held, only experienced. It cannot be touched, only felt. It cannot be seen, only glimpsed, with the inner eye. The term Tao is an attempt to put into words what is wordless, to give sound to the great silence. For the Tao is our source, our path, our end as it is our beginning.

The Chinese character for Tao is made of two characters, one meaning to follow and another representing the face of a human being; it illustrates a person following a path. Tao is that path.

Like Western science, Western alchemy, and to a certain extent Indian practical philosophy, the beginning of Taoism lies in observation. With Taoism the principle model is Nature.

Thousands of years ago, observers noted a principle that worked in Nature, and in the body of the human observing Nature. The observers noted that there was a flow to nature that when mirrored in their bodies — and the actions of their bodies, minds, and spirits — led to a spiritual awakening. This was the Tao, or *Dao*, roughly translated as *the flow*.

These observers also studied animals – how they moved, the positions they took when resting, the plants they ate when they were sick or injured. They experimented; eating the plants they saw animals eating and then combining them in various ways. By observing the seasons, the flow of each one into and out of the other, they learned the patterns and texture of time. They observed the dance of the stars and planets in the sky and how they seemed to affect human behavior. They looked deeply into themselves and observed the waxing and waning of their own energy and how that seemed to flow in certain pathways of their bodies.

Shen Nong, the father of Chinese herbalism, whose work, the *Shen Nong Ben Cao Jing* or *Shen Nong's Herbal Classic*, was one of these observers. He observed herbs and medicines and built a collection of remedies. His book lists 365 formulas and herbal preparations derived from plant, animal and mineral sources and is still used today.

The interesting thing about Shen Nong is his use of personal observation. He is said to have tasted each herb or medicine personally. Apparently, he was poisoned many times. But fortunately, he also consumed so many beneficial herbs and medicines that he was able to recover each time.

The flow in nature observed by these people in ancient times was also called *wu wei*, meaning *without action*. To further elucidate this idea, the adepts of the Tao, including Lao Tzu, used the paradox *wei wu wei*, that is, *action without action.*

The Watercourse Way is probably the name that communicates this principle best. Imagine a soft flow of water tumbling over a jagged chunk of granite day after day. Eventually, through persistence, the water wears down the rock, rounding the corners, making the flow easier and smoother.

This illustrates a main idea of Taoism. Soft measures can overcome hard barriers. Obstacles in your life can be overcome with creativity and persistence. Assuming the humble quality of a drop of water, you can use flexibility and adaptability to solve your problems. It isn't necessary to blast the rocks away. By taking time to think like the gentle stream of water moving through a harsh environment, you can find a flow that takes you around, over, or under anything that blocks your path. Like water, you must be patient. After all, change is inevitable.

It is in this ability to flow like water, to take the shape of whatever container you find yourself in, to adapt to any physical obstacle, following the path of least resistance that, "by doing nothing," you can achieve Tao.

Lao Tzu said:

Under heaven nothing is more soft and yielding than water.
yet for attacking the solid and strong, nothing is better;
it has no equal.
The weak can overcome the strong;
the supple can overcome the stiff.
Under heaven everyone knows this,
yet few put it into practice.
Chapter 78

Wu wei is a fundamental principle that teaches that going against the flow, or against Nature, or even against your own nature, will only result in problems. Like spitting into the wind, when you try to push your agenda and *force* things to happen, you set yourself up for failure. In wu wei, you become sensitive to each moment and your place in it and then act accordingly. It can only be learned by becoming patient and non-attached to what you *want* to happen instead of what really *is* happening. Then, finding a way to be happy with what is happening, you will be able to flow with it in a graceful and harmonious manner. You can drift contentedly in the universe. In this way, it is a very powerful tool in spiritual self-cultivation.

The ultimate reality for you then is that the real you is the Tao. You are one with the universe, inseparable. Realizing the Tao is becoming a self realized human being (*zhen ren*).

Of course, the beauty of Taoism is that it's a natural, flowing, flexible method of self-realization. It's a dance where you can change the music to your whim. It's an individual experience with an ultimate goal of enjoyment and appreciation of the present moment, with all due consideration and love for other expressions of the Tao.

Still, it's also good to remember that the true Tao is something indescribable and inexpressible. It's something you can't really define and pin down, but rather just is.

It is all in the personal experience. The Taoist path is a body-centered path. In other words, even though there were schools of Taoism such as the Shangqing, which contained "out of body" ecstatic wandering, Taoist practices focus on using the physical body. Taoists work with the "field of elixirs", the *dan tians*. The upper dan tian is in the third eye region, the middle dan tian is in the heart center and the lower dan tian is in the lower abdomen. There are also various energy points along the major qi pathways of the body. These are all ways to use our own internal energy to hook up to the vast, ever shifting energy of the Tao itself.

Unlike Buddhists and Hindus, Taoists do not see the outer world of nature as illusory, or at least not in the same way. Nature is not *maya* (illusion). You can observe the elements of Nature.

And even though everything is real, it's still mostly not what it mostly seems to be. You can work with Nature and with your own natural self to obtain a spiritual harmony and spiritual truth.

Taoism ultimately sees Nature reflected in the body. Taoism wants the body treated with respect and for it to be as it should; healthy, harmonious, and at peace.

Another vital principle in the human body, which is reflected in Nature, is that of opposite forces. Taoists noted that within humanity, as within all living things in Nature, there were males and there were females. But more complicated than that, there were male and female aspects in both sexes. They discovered that this was mirrored in the nature of the universe itself.

They called these forces in bodies and in the universe yin and yang.

The ancient Taoists, those natural philosophers of change and balance, used the concepts of yin and yang to symbolize the polarity of existence. Everything that exists can be assigned either to yin or yang, thus identifying its polar aspects. In this way, all elements are paired and balanced with each other – night and day, sun and moon, moist and dry, dark and light, fire and water. It is through this interdependence and interrelationship that the universe, and we humans within it, remain in balance and harmony.

Solala Towler [1]

The yin/yang symbol is well known even now in the Western world. It's a circle with a backward "S" running from top to bottom. To the left it's white. To the right it's black. In the white part at the top part, there's a small circle, colored black. There's a corresponding small white circle below in the black. The white part is yang. The black part is yin.

1 *Embarking on the Way* by Solala Towler, Abode of the Eternal Tao,1997.

The white part, or yang, symbolizes the male or masculine aspect of the whole. The black part, yin, symbolizes the female or feminine aspect of the whole. In truth, this symbol should be represented, not as yin and yang but as yin/yang as they are both parts of the same whole, not two different things.

Yin and yang are the antitheses of phenomena in the natural world, combining to create a unity of opposites.

Visualize a mountain as the sun sets in the evening. One side of the mountain is bathed in radiant sunshine; the other side is in shadow. However, though having both dark and light sides, this mountain is still a cohesive force in and of itself. There is no conflict between the light and the dark; just different shades of the same formation.

Yin Yang or Great Ultimate (Taiji) Symbol

Yang is brightness, creation, activity and heat. It's the sky, and the constant stars.

Yin is darkness, receptivity, passivity, peace and the cool acceptance of the earth.

The Taoists observed these principles in Nature as they also observed the balance between them. Moreover, they observed these opposite forces in their own bodies. There is a unified whole; a unified field. It is composed of active and inactive components, in constant flux.

Imagine a beach at low tide and then again at high tide. On the same beach, but at low tide, there are seaweed strands clinging to rocks and tide pools with stranded starfish and sea anemone gently waving fronds under shallow water. At high tide, the waves crash on smooth hot sand. It's a different view, but of the same thing. You see different parts of the same whole.

Or, imagine the warp and woof underlying the weave of the foundation of Nature, like the opposing directional weave of the same cloth on a loom.

And what about those circles of dark in the light, and light in the dark in the symbols for yin/yang? Every man has a feminine side and vice versa. Sometimes a man shows his softer nature; sometimes a woman shows her tougher side.

The principle of polarity is to be found everywhere in the universe. For example, the earth moves and rhythmically changes its position in relation to the sun. This brings about the slow change from day and daylight through the dusk into the darkness of night. The interplay of change and movement of yin and yang brings about every change and every movement in the universe.

All things, yin and yang, are in One. Yet all things have one infinite source, the Void, or Zero. And there are definite patterns in nature; in all things.

The Chinese view the human body as a microcosm of the universe, reflecting the relationships seen in the cosmos. They believe that the same energy that rules the universe and breathes life into Nature also has a determining influence on humans. Chinese philosophy regards humans as part of the cosmos, embedded in the rhythms of the universe, a fulcrum between heaven and earth.

It would seem that Taoism itself is derived from a systems theory that attempts to quantify and explain patterns in the universe. This is the *I Ching* (*Yi Jing*). Certainly it was a main source of inspiration for Confucius and Lao Tzu.

The *I Ching* (or *Book of Changes* or, better, *Classic of Changes*) is well known these days, yet generally misunderstood. Look for this book in your bookstore, and it's likely to be filed away in the divination section alongside tarot cards.

In fact, the *I Ching* is a system that attempts to peer into chance events in order to establish some kind of understanding, to put them into some kind of order, to explain or map out the circumstances of life, it is

106

an explanation of patterns.

The *I Ching* contained the first printed use of yin and yang and the symbol for yin and yang. It centers on the dynamic balance of these opposites, the process of events in an evolutionary sense, all with the acceptance of change in mind. The investigators and creators of these systems used the observation of male and female energies in the human body.

Like the abacus, it's an ancient computer, used to understand and perceive reality. The abacus has used beans, stone, or beads in grooves, on tablets, or on strings for calculations; combining patterns along a straight line.

The *I Ching,* on the other hand, is a system of hexagrams. One may use yarrow stalks, coins, seeds, or even computer-generated symbols, to cast the *I Ching*, while addressing a particular question. The question is given about a present situation, looking for a yes or no answer with branching possibilities. The resultant configuration is then compared with correlating interpretations. Naturally, the conclusions are open for interpretation, presumably using one's harmony with the Tao.

Although commonly used to ask such questions as whether or not to change a job, the *I Ching* is an embodiment of Chinese philosophy and wisdom with a rich history and richer uses. While on the surface a tool of divination, there was much more behind its use. The *I Ching* can be best seen as a kind of psychological and philosophical exploration of chance events as interpreted by the systems of Nature and the body, discerned by wise observers.

Contemporary Taoist master Ni Hua Ching suggested that the *Book of Changes* teaches one to look for the most appropriate point in any particular event or behavior. It can be quite useful for self-discovery and aligning the self. [2]

When you gain that sense of appropriateness, you find yourself aligned with natural laws or patterns. This is helpful in all spheres of life, giving you mental clarity, physical balance, and positive spiritual growth.

So, what does the *I Ching* have to do with the body and opening up the portals of enlightenment and freedom?

The *I Ching* and Taoism gave birth to the procedures and systems that formulated all the other Chinese systems that work with the human

---

2 *The Book of Changes and the Unchanging Truth* by Hua Ching Ni, SevenStar Communications, 1990.

body. Its principles underlie the practical application of philosophy for both medical and spiritual purposes.

And, while the *I Ching* is often used for divination purposes, another very important aspect of working with the *Book of Changes* is for self-cultivation practice. Taoists liken spiritual work to creating and tending a garden. You plant the seeds of spiritual fruit that you wish to harvest and then you watch over them with tender care, watering them with tears of joy and sorrow and fertilizing them with challenges and opportunities in your life. In time, and with enough care, this garden will grow and flourish.

With the guidance of the *I Ching* you can better understand where you are in any given moment in time. You can notice the various factors or influences that are all coming together in this moment. You learn what is appropriate for this time. In this way you are better able to make decisions about how to act or not act, if this is a time to move forward or backward or to stand still, whether this is a time of strength for you or a sign that you need to husband your energy so that you can build up your qi reserves and move forward when the time is right.

As the Chinese understood, great spiritual growth can be possible in times of the greatest adversity and challenges. If you know how to respond appropriately, you can experience huge leaps in spiritual awareness.

Taoist masters suggest that the nature of personal problems and the entirety of the universe can be perceived by studying the subtle spiritual levels of the *I Ching*.

An old saying about the *I Ching* states that it is a means "to understand the heart of the mind, see the Original Spirit and arrive at destiny." Its ancient emphasis was on seeing the Original Face or Entering the Tao.

Clearly the earliest creators of Taoism were some of the greatest observers and thinkers. One of the major authors of Taoism, in fact, was also credited with the creation of the Chinese medical system, probably the oldest system of alchemy in the world.

This was the Yellow Emperor (Huang Di), the same royal personage who is attributed with formulating the techniques of sexual yoga, given to him by three female adepts. *The Yellow Emperor's Classic of Internal Medicine* is the first medical treatise in the history of China and is still used today.

He lived a very long time ago, variously given as 2697 to 2597 BCE or 2674 to 2574 BCE. This was a period of amazing creativity and innovation. The Yellow Emperor himself is credited with the invention of writing, the compass, the pottery wheel, and the art of breeding silk worms.

There is a traditional story about the Yellow Emperor which describes his birth as a spontaneous result of the fusion of energies that marked the beginning of the world. He then created humans as earthen statues, each standing at the cardinal points of the world. For three hundred years, these statues stood immobile, exposed to the breath of the world's beginning. When they were totally pervaded by the energy of this breath, the statues began to speak and move. This was how the races of humans were formed.

According to legend, the Yellow Emperor attained immortality at the age of 100. He possessed magical powers and produced the golden elixir, *chin-tan*. At his death, he was taken up to heaven, leaving behind only his clothing and cap to be entombed. He ascended into heaven riding a dragon and became ruler of the center of the five cardinal points.

Notice the resemblance between the Yellow Emperor's riding off to heaven on the back of a dragon and Jesus Christ's ascension into heaven. It seems that Eastern culture and Western culture both may have been based upon men who achieved the Rainbow Body. Resemblances continue. The Yellow Emperor represents the ideal of the philosopher king or shaman king whose family forms both the genetic and cultural ancestry of a civilization. Jesus, coming from the seed of David and Abraham, fulfilled both a genetic link as the Son of Man, and a cultural prophecy as the Messiah, Son of God.

That the Yellow Emperor, who embodies the cultural ancestry of the Chinese civilization, is also attributed as the source of Chinese Medicine is no surprise. The Chinese traditional medicine system is intertwined with spiritual cultivation and techniques for spiritual awakening. It is based as much on inner illuminations as on longevity.

The Chinese observed that the body is composed of a pre-birth and a post-birth energy system, which is separated at the time of birth. The human body is viewed as the harmonious union of yin and yang. Good health is based upon the smooth flow of yin and yang throughout the body. This energy can be increased though specific practices. Proper cultivation results in greatly increased strength, endurance and agility.

The Neijing Tu Map is an ancient chart showing the inner meridians or channels, where qi flows in the body. Note how the chart resembles a fetus or meditator. As an inner landscape with trees and mountains, it portrays the microcosm of nature. At the base of the spine is found a water wheel, run by two children on a treadmill, representing yin and yang. The eyes are labeled sun and moon.

This process of increasing the power and health of the body primarily through breathing and qi exercises, as well as with herbs and acupuncture, is the basis of the Chinese medical system. It's also the foundation of the Chinese martial arts tradition, which was originally based on shamanism. Chinese medicine unites alchemy, shamanism and yoga into a single clear and coherent system, which has a direct correspondence with Tibetan, Indian and Western alchemical systems of spiritual transmutation.

The internal alchemy system creates an inner elixir by developing the soul from three energies: jing, qi, and shen. Jing is the essence. Qi is vital energy. Shen refers to the spirit. The physical body system works with various chemical substances to keep the body alive, and also make an elixir of immortality through correct amounts of fluids, neurotransmitters, and cell functions, for instance. In inner alchemy practices (*nei dan*), the essence of jing combines with the life force of qi to fashion the Immortal Embryo, with the help of the mind. The practice of nei dan creates the Immortal Embryo from the inner alchemical process and by taming the thought processes of the mind. All processes that could possibly lead to a person's death can be reversed by focusing and purifying the life energies within the body, making them independent of the sensory world.

The Immortal Embryo is fashioned within a human being by practicing various meditative breathing techniques. Also known as the Golden Flower, it opens or is realized when the practitioner attains enlightenment. This spiritual awakening, seeing the Golden Embryo, consists of a return to nothingness, or the void. By balancing yin and yang in the body, you become one with the Tao.

During the Sung Dynasty, the inner elixir practices of nei dan, and the school of the Realization of Truth (Chuan-chen Taoism) gained popularity. Its various branches have been strongly influenced by Buddhism, especially Zen (called Chan in China).

Zen Buddhism is a powerful system of Buddhism, imported to Japan through the alchemy of Chinese philosophy. The founder of Zen Buddhism in China was called Bodhidharma in India, or Da Mo in China. Stories tell that he started on a long journey from India to China at the age of 64. He brought with him new teachings, which centered

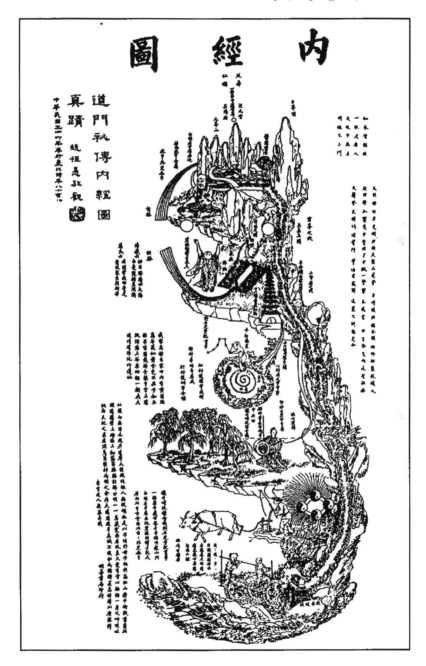

on a sitting meditation called Chan. Later, when the samurai class in Japan began using this technique it was called Zen.

When Da Mo first arrived in China, he was granted an audience with Emperor Wu, who was anxious to question him about his Indian Buddhist knowledge. From his royal presence on the Dragon Throne, Emperor Wu described all the temples he had erected and boasted of the many ceremonies and rituals that he had sponsored. He expected some impressive response from Da Mo who just stared at him without comment. So Emperor Wu asked Da Mo what his opinion was of the value of his many works.

Da Mo replied, "None."

Disappointed, Emperor Wu next queried Da Mo as to the basic teaching of Buddhism.

Da Mo answered, "Vast emptiness."

Emperor Wu shouted at the bedraggled figure in front of him, "Just who do you think you are?"

Da Mo said, "I have no idea." He then turned and left the palace, going to a cave in nearby mountains where he meditated for many years.

Long periods of meditation can give excellent experiences. The simple technique of just being in the moment is powerful. Practicing mindfulness in daily life also has good results. However, prolonged sitting meditations need to be balanced with techniques that involve body movement. In China there is an old saying that a hinge that is never used will rust and become stuck but one that is used constantly will always remain smooth and flexible.

Da Mo saw the ill health of the monks who had spent years in sitting meditation and introduced a form of martial arts movement now called Shaolin. Similarly, the body centered traditions of qi gong, tai chi, and martial arts bring the body back into balance necessary for good health and long life.

In the Chan-influenced School of the Realization of Truth, inner alchemy texts recorded teachings such as the Secret of the Golden Flower practice. The main teaching was that there are three human vital energies; jing, qi, and shen. These energies have a material and visible aspect, which is active within the physical body. At the same time, they have an immaterial, invisible aspect, which is active within the universe

Da Mo (Bodhidharma)

Yoshitoshi, 1887

Practitioners of inner alchemy work at creating the inner elixir by purifying the essence of jing, which comes from reproductive energy at the starting point of the body, transforming it into the vital energy of qi, purifying the qi, and transforming that into shen, or spirit. This is done by a variety of yogic techniques that work by increasing the inner heat of the body. The final stage of the nei dan school is to purify the mind and return to the void, integrating the self with the universe. This is sometimes called "shattering space."

The strengthening of one's own essence is necessary for the successful practice of nei dan. Sexual yoga was one technique employed to conserve the energy lost in male orgasms during sexual intercourse. Not all paths accepted this practice.

The actual work of the inner alchemist begins with working with the channels within the body in which vital energy can circulate. The first of these is called lesser celestial circulation, which begins at the perineum and rises from the lower end of the spine along the vertebral column to the top of the head and from there over the face, chest, and abdominal surface, back down to the end of the lower abdomen (dan tian).

As this current of energy ascends it is called the governing vessel. As it descends it is called the conception vessel. The ascent and descent together are the fusion of yang and yin, in which the goal of nei dan is realized.

In inner alchemy practice, it is taught that attaining the Tao can only be achieved through the union of two inner bodies, the yin (tiger) and yang (dragon) of the Chinese system, and the mother and child lights of the *Mahamudra* and *Ati* Yoga systems of Tibet.

Same truths are told in different words. The union of opposites can be called a union of dragon and tiger, the combination of yin and yang. It is the subtle body embracing the super subtle body. All describe the spiritual awakening as understood in each culture's spiritual metaphors.

There is also a pathway in the Chinese martial arts, as with other heat-producing techniques, that works to raise the qi, awaken the kundalini, and eventually see the Original Face, the Golden Embryo.

This is the Golden Flower of Chinese alchemy.

KEY CONCEPTS
- Taoism is an eloquent system toward enlightenment or self-realization, developed by the ancient Chinese.
- Taoism focuses on a central vital force that runs through the universe, better experienced than described.
- Taoist masters developed physical and mental practices that harnessed this force toward health, vitality and longevity.
- Uniting yin and yang within the body results in the discovery that the microcosm of the body actually contains the macrocosm of the universe.

CHAPTER FOURTEEN
The Three Treasures and the Golden Embryo
An Experience of Chinese Alchemy

Ancestor Lu, a Taoist alchemist, suggested that what is assumed to be physical – the human body – in its ideal form consists of the Three Treasures – vitality, energy and spirit.

The first of these Three Treasures is *jing*. In Sanskrit it is *bindu;* in Tibetan it is *thigle*. It is also sometimes referred to as prenatal qi and is a combination of the qi of both of our parents at the moment of conception.

This is one of the reasons that, in Taoist thought, sexual activity is not advised if both or even one of the parents is under the influence of alcohol, seriously unhealthy, or emotionally unstable. This would result in the baby being born with poor jing, and hence be born with a poor constitution.

Jing regulates our hormonal and reproductive systems, controls our growth throughout life, and regulates our central nervous system, including the brain, spinal cord and bone marrow. It also governs our constitution. Jing is said to reside in our kidneys and is also the repository of our creative and sexual energy.

Another role of jing is linked to the aging process. Too much loss of sexual essence, or jing, in men through incorrect sexual habits leads to faster aging. This is one of the reasons you may see more women than men in retirement homes or assisted living centers; women far outlive men.

The second Treasure is qi. In Sanskrit it is *prana;* in Tibetan it is *lung.*

Qi can be thought of as basic life force, or vital energy. It is what animates us, what gives us life. It warms us, keeps our organs in place and directs all our movements.

Not only that but there are different kinds of qi; for instance, organ qi and protective or *wei* qi, among others. Modern Chinese even refer to the weather as a kind of qi.

One of the more familiar types of qi, accessed during acupuncture treatments, is meridian qi. This type of qi travels throughout our body in specific pathways or meridians, linking organs to each other. This is what acupuncturists tap into when they insert needles.

You get qi from the air you breathe, the food you eat and the water you drink. This is why it is so important to eat fresh, high quality food. Eating too many processed foods, with little qi in them, will produce poor qi in your body.

Qi can also be thought of as electricity. It can't be seen but it can be felt, even measured. You can even think of your meridian system as an electrical system complete with junctures, fuse boxes, and miles of wiring, all connecting in one great multi-level energy circuit.

There are also other kinds of qi – emotional qi, spiritual qi, even thinking qi. The act of writing this book and you reading it, produces a kind of qi connection by communicating information which you receive.

There is also primordial qi, the original animating, creative force of the universe.

Master Hua Ching Ni, physician, co-founder of a school of Traditional Chinese Medicine, and teacher of Tao philosophy, describes the universe as alive. "It is the continual transformation of primal qi, the pivotal energy and living soul of the universe." [1]

Primal qi connects the universe just as the nervous system interacts within the human body. It is the basic natural force of the universe. All things in the universe are the same, just different nuances of qi. Or as ancient sages have said, "All things are one, and the one is all things."

All transformation is the result of the exchange of qi, forward or backward.

The last of the Three Treasures is *shen*, also called spirit or consciousness. It is what gives our lives meaning and links us with our divine source. Shen is said to reside in the heart and to open through the eyes; as in "The eyes are the mirrors of the soul."

A Western doctor shines a light in your eyes, not just looking for cataracts, but taking advantage of the opening that gives a direct view of the condition of your retinal blood vessels. Seeing them clearly in the back of your eye, the doctor has some idea of the condition of your blood vessels in general.

A doctor of Chinese medicine can tell the seriousness of a condition by looking into the patient's eyes. Bright or clear eyes indicate that the shen or spirit is strong; then the chances of recovery are good. Clouded, glazed or unfocused eyes indicate a more doubtful prognosis.

To the Chinese, the mind also resides in the heart. Follow your

---

1 *The Book of Changes and the Unchanging Truth* by Hua Ching Ni, SevenStar Communications, 1992.

heart, learning by heart, listening to your heart – these all come from this belief. These sayings are also used in the West, hinting at the same heart/mind connection.

Ancestor Lu considered the spirit to reside in an alchemical storehouse. If secure, the spirit was calm. The spirit controlled the vitality of the body, crystallizing the Great Elixir, creating the Immortal Embryo.

The original self is obscured by the senses. Seeing a beautiful sunset, you forget to see who you really are. Hearing a rousing symphony by Tchaikovsky, you forget. Tasting a pungent curry sauce, you forget. Smelling the deep sweetness of a red rose, you forget. Pounding the earth, jogging through a park, your body forgets who it really is. Once the senses are removed, the true self emerges.

It's been said by some that a good way to see differently is to shift the focus of consciousness back just a bit into the brain from where it is now. So, as you look at these words, think about where you seem to live behind your eyes. Now move this focal point back an inch or two. If you can do this exercise regularly with a quiet mind and slowed breathing, you can achieve a shift in consciousness. This is because you're actually shifting your sense of consciousness back to where the seat of consciousness – the third eye (upper dan tian), the pineal gland – resides. This technique will help you think about consciousness and its nature, how it leads you to wonderful places, and yet how the very nature of your senses distracts you from who you truly are.

An ancient Taoist text called the *Huainanzi*, describes this process:

When the mind (the will) is concentrated on the inside of the body, it can pervade everything just as the One or the Tao itself. As long as the mind stays unmoving, one will never know what one is doing, nor where one is going…The body is like a withered tree, the mind is like cold ashes. The five orbs and the body itself are beyond one's thoughts, one knows without studying, sees without looking, accomplishes things without doing anything. Without throwing light on things one will find them clear, pushed along one will move, instinctively one will go on – flowingly, as the shadow follows the light.

Hidemi Ishida [2]

2 *Taoist Meditation and Longevity Techniques*, edited by Livia Kohn, Michigan Monographs. in Chinese Studies, 1989.

In ancient Taoist texts this practice is known as "fasting of the heart." The idea here is that by stilling the mind the practitioner is calming the *shen*, which, remember, resides in the heart.

The ancient Taoist philosopher, Chuang Tzu, describes it like this:

You must center your heart/mind in perfect harmony. Do not listen with your ears but with your heart/mind. Do not listen with your heart/mind but with your vital energy (qi). Hearing stops with the ears, thoughts and ideas stop with the mind. Your qi or vital energy though, resides in stillness and is open and receptive to all things. True knowledge or Tao, resides in stillness and emptiness and to attain this emptiness one must use the fasting of the mind. [3]

How exactly does one proceed in this "fasting of the mind" practice?

First sit quietly, away from external noises like traffic, television, and people talking. Then focus on your breath. If thoughts come because of stresses in life, let them unfold and process, and then let them go. Fantasies and random thoughts should be discarded. Return to focus on your breath. You will create a state of mind that is at peace, detached from external senses. You will hear but pay no mind to what you hear, as if you had heard nothing.

Lao Tzu says:

Allow yourself to become empty.
Abide in stillness.
The ten thousand beings rise and flourish
while the sage watches their return.
Though all beings exist in profusion
they all end up returning to their source.
Returning to their source is called tranquility.
This is called "returning to their original nature."
   Chapter 16

Another term for Taoist meditation is "sitting and forgetting." By sitting quietly and allowing all outside influences to fade away and all inner thoughts to flow by without grasping and without attachment, your body becomes "like a withered tree" and your mind "is like cold ashes."

Even though these images may seem a bit grim this state is actually

3 *Chuang Tzu: The Inner Chapters* by Solala Towler, Watkins Publishing, 2010.

one of complete detachment and inner quiet. This is the first important stage of internal alchemy. If you are not able to sit quietly while breathing deeply and slowly, you will not be able to attain the higher levels of nei dan practice.

The next level is to be able to maintain this meditative state in all activities. While walking, standing, eating, drinking, sleeping, and resting, you continue to meditate. Keeping your breath and your essence intact, the spirit remains in the body, increasing longevity.

If you are able to maintain this quiet mind/spirit in all of your activities then you will be able to go on to the higher levels of nei dan practice, the Immortal Embryo or the Golden Elixir.

The ancient Taoists believed there is an indescribable something, Tao, running through the universe like a fuse. The secret to enlightenment and ultimate freedom is to dissolve one's self into Tao, surrender to it to achieve longevity, health, and balance.

Time after time, though, the Taoists talk about their goal of living in their bodies forever. Legends, such as those about the Eight Immortals, support that idea.

Even scientists today suggest that, according to what we know now about the way the body ages and why, technology a hundred years from now will allow individuals born then to live hundreds of years.

The vital lessons of the ancient Taoists are much more practical and applicable to you. The Taoist alchemists basically said that you can use your body as a foundation for achieving enlightenment.

Chinese alchemy, in ancient texts, teaches that the cosmos is the final stage in a series of spontaneous transmutations stemming from original non-existence. Primeval unity is a union of opposites, generating the cosmos.

The ultimate goal of the Chinese alchemist is the achievement of the Golden Elixir. This is the stuff of which enlightenment is made!

According to the alchemists, the process was very much like the process described in the awakening of the kundalini through tantric methods. The jing is cultivated and preserved in the lower torso in a firing process like the concept of tapas used in yoga. Jing is heated by an inner heat and it rises up through channels known as *nadis* in Sanskrit. Once it reaches the top region of the body, this process opens up new vistas through the third eye. The individual is then able to look upon his Original Face, his Golden Embryo, or what Ancestor Lu calls the Primordial.

To revisit and summarize the essential formula for attaining the completion state of Chinese alchemy and realizing the Tao – you refine jing into qi, qi into shen, return shen to the void, and return the void to Tao. Or, another way to say that is to refine your essence into vital energy, vital energy into spirit, and return the spirit to the void. When shen is returned to the void, the yin and yang subtle bodies have embraced. When the void is returned to Tao, it is called "shattering space." You have seen the Golden Embryonic version of yourself dissolve into nothingness.

In body-centered Taoism, the physical body is valued, in contrast to Hindu or ascetic renunciation practices which attach no value to the physical body. Longevity is prized because it takes many, many years to refine the Three Treasures and particularly to refine shen, the spirit hidden within the body.

Mixing ingredients together transforms the original elements and, as with a recipe, achieves a known result. When you heat egg yolks, sugar, vanilla and cream and cool it, you have made a custard. When you add flour, salt, milk, baking powder, and cook it in a pan in the oven you have made something entirely different, a cake. Kitchen alchemy is the province of all good chefs.

Alchemy of any kind can be defined as the seemingly magical process of transmuting one substance into another substance of greater value. It's been described, for example, as the process of turning lead into gold. There have always been those adherents of alchemy who were concerned with mastering the outer world in such a way, and they approached physical security and longevity as an outside-in process. Their pursuits led to discoveries such as gunpowder, and eventually developed into chemistry and modern day pharmacology.

When you see fireworks exploding on the Fourth of July, you can see evidence of the results of outer alchemy.

Inner alchemy is living in a continuum of spirit, in a proper alchemical mix of body and spirit. The goal is the union of Heaven, Earth, and Humanity.

Without proper balance in outer alchemy, you see the oceans become great dumpsites for humanity's discarded material. You see oil spills and oil seepages.

The environmental movement is the outer alchemical movement towards balancing the needs of humans with the precious gifts of mother Earth. It is right to have concern regarding industrial pollutants in our air

120

and water. The effect of changes in water temperature upsets the balance of life in the oceans and weather patterns, which, in turn, transforms the experience of the entire world. The balance of nature is upset when the ozone layer develops holes and the ice caps melt.

All adherents to the inner branch of alchemy are devoted to activating what the Indians called kundalini and the Chinese called the Immortal Embryo or Golden Flower, in order to achieve enlightenment or realization of the Tao.

This alchemical process is sometimes described as the refining of elements of the body with the mind, and awakening the latent spiritual content, and refining it into the "gold" of spirit.

The process begins with the spiritual or subtle gold, which exists within every human being. This subtle gold comes into form with the initial spark of life at an individual's conception, prior to gender differentiation.

After a human sperm wiggles into an egg, and the resultant zygote becomes implanted safely in the wall of the uterus, there is a period of time when the fetus is neither male nor female, but both. It is androgynous. This embryonic "gold," which we have also called "the starting point of the body," stays in the body. It lies in a dormant state until activated through qi raising techniques such as yoga, tai chi, qi gong, and meditation.

Through transformation and integration the alchemist achieves realization. At this point, the practitioner becomes aware and has access to universal consciousness – cosmic consciousness. It also results in the beginning of tremendous physical rejuvenation and health benefits. Your superpowers await your alchemical work to generate your own immortality.

In Taoist alchemy, an Immortal is a person who achieves the completion stage of alchemy and has fully refined all three forces – jing, qi and shen – into a functional state of total multi-dimensional awareness. In this way, they exist beyond time and space and are thus immortal.

The process of working with jing, qi and shen is one of transformation – from the gross level of jing up through the more refined energy of qi and then to the even more refined energy of shen or pure spirit. Then there is one more layer of refinement, back to the primordial Tao or Wu Ji, the universe.

The Chinese system, unlike other cultivation techniques of the East and West, uses the body as the starting point. These practices are not geared toward getting the practitioner up and out of the body, but instead turn you inward and downward.

Lao Tzu advised, "Know the yang but hold to the yin." In other words, honor the yang or upward, outward, dynamic energy but the real key in self cultivation is to work with the yin aspect, which is connected to the earth, to water, to the dark mystery of the yin principle.

Indeed, the quest to become a Taoist Immortal was said to involve both body as well as the mind. In this system, the body is revered. Without the body in which to ground the spiritual/energetic practices the practitioner can easily be led into body-negating ascetic practices, those same practices that the Buddha rejected. Good health and longevity indicate mastery over the physical body and complement the realization of the spirit body.

Many of the qi gong techniques practiced today were originally created, like many of the yogic practices of India, to strengthen the body and energy system of the practitioner so that she could then go on to the more subtle refinements of internal alchemy.

There is a story of a devoted practitioner of the Taoist arts who was frustrated in the lack of progress after years of earnest efforts. One day, an Immortal appeared to him and told him that he was ill and would never find success unless his health was restored. The adept began taking care of his body with proper food, sleep and exercise after which he had amazing experiences.

Outer practice is done to maintain health, flexibility and strength, which are all good things, but the most powerful alchemical practices involve quiet sitting (*zuowanglun*) with energy activation.

If you ask a Taoist master even today what is the highest, most powerful practice of self cultivation they will not tell you kung fu or tai chi or even qi gong. Quiet sitting is what they will say. Of course what looks on the outside like someone sitting quietly and immobile can be deceiving. On the inside the practitioner will be moving energy either in the Small Circulation (up the back and down the front) or else in the Large Circulation with energy going to all parts of the body.

As mentioned before, Taoist alchemy involves a process or refinement or transformation of gross energy into ever more pure realms until the practitioner reaches the level of Wu Ji, the Primordial. Then it will be up to him or her whether they will remain in the physical world, or "fly off to heaven on the back of a dragon," or even travel back and forth from one world to the other.

But all these spiritual travels and experiences begin with the foundation practice of breath, intent, and focus – usually beginning with the practice already described. It is in creating a firm and solid foundation, energetically and spiritually, that you can then build ever higher into the rarified air of the purely spiritual, where the physical no longer has a hold on you and where you can "live off dew and air," like the Immortals written about in ancient Chinese texts.

Meditation has long been used as a tool for achieving inner harmony by many cultures. Taoist meditation can be done in various ways – moving, standing, sitting or even lying down.

The goal of meditation is to achieve a level or experience of peacefulness, relaxation and the opening of one's deeper or higher nature.

Lao Tzu says:

The Tao does not act
yet there is nothing that it does not achieve.
If princes and kings could uphold this
then everything would develop naturally.
If they still desire to act
they should themselves return
to the formless beginning.
Without form there is no desire
and with no desire
things return to tranquility.
Then all under heaven
will naturally calm themselves.
Chapter 37

By creating an atmosphere of detachment to the comings and goings of the world, to the ten thousand beings, you will not get so caught up in the distractions of the world and, instead, find a place of peace and tranquility.

By slowing down, by watching your breath, by allowing your mind to move more slowly and deeply, you can reach new levels of understanding about yourself as well as the world around you.

The first and fundamental practice is one of bringing the fire of the heart (shen) down to the water of the kidneys (jing) and heating that water up in the cauldron of the lower dantian or field of elixir, located in the lower abdomen. By "cooking" this substance in this alchemical fashion the practitioner is able to refine his or her qi to a much purer state.

Here's another description of this process, from an ancient Taoist text.

...your pure yang qi is born after the essence is refined and made into an elixir. After you refine the qi and complete the Spirit, the Realized Numinous Divine Immortal transcends the ordinary and enters into sacredness. You abandon your shell and ascend to immortality and this is called "transcending and escaping," This is the method of divine immortals that has not changed for a hundred million years!

Stephen Eskildsen [4]

The actual practice is quite simple and can be done by anyone. It is for the higher levels that you need a teacher or guide as altering your qi can create all sorts of special effects energetically and can be confusing or even painful if you do it incorrectly. The fundamental practice though, is done by putting your attention or focus on your lower dantian (actually one third of the way inside the body just under the navel) during meditation.

So begins the first step in the alchemical process to reach that alchemical gold. Once awakened and properly brought up through the body to activate the pineal gland, this alchemical process transforms the alchemist.

Sit, either on a cushion or the edge of a chair. Then, either close your eyes or keep them open only slightly. Breathe slowly and deeply, through your nose, and from your belly, using your diaphragm to really fill your lungs, from the bottom up. As you inhale allow your abdomen to expand. Then, as you exhale, allow it to contract. In Taoist practice, this is called "natural breathing."

Now concentrate your internal vision upon the space below your navel, in the lower torso. This space is called the lower dantian or "field of elixir." By concentrating on this space you will be able to build a strong foundation of qi or internal energy.

Begin by counting your breaths on each inhale and exhale. Start by counting up to ten and then begin again. This will help your mind to

4 *The Teachings and Practices of the Early Quanzhen Taoist Masters* by Stephen Eskildsen, State University of New York Press, 2004.

have something to concentrate on as thoughts pass through when you begin meditating.

As you inhale, breathe in clear or golden light or healing qi. Feel it enter every cell of your body, filling it with light. After practicing in this way for some time you will feel heat or tingling in that area. This will eventually begin to permeate your whole body and is the first step in the alchemical transformation of jing, qi and shen.

Then, as you exhale, let go of all tensions, toxins, pain or any negative energy you feel in your body. Feel it flowing out of you like dark smoke.

As you inhale allow that golden light or healing qi to enter your body. Feel it flowing into your whole body, into every dark corner. If you have disease or pain, allow that healing qi to flow to that part of your body and envelop it in healing light.

End the meditation by briskly rubbing the palms of your hands together, either 36 times or as long as it takes to produce some heat. Then lay your palms over your eyes and breathe the heat from the *lao gong* points in your hands into your eyes. Then rub your face a few times, gently, up and down.

Be easy in re-entering the world immediately after a meditation session. Move slowly and savor the peaceful feelings you have created. You may be very sensitive or emotionally open at this time and can be easily affected by the negative energy of the world outside your door or of another person. Give yourself some time to acclimate.

Another form of meditation, called sitting in tranquility, is just to sit and breathe, thinking of nothing, envisioning nothing. Merely sit and let yourself "be breathed." In this way you allow yourself time to simply *be*. This can have a wonderfully rejuvenating effect on both your body and your spirit.

Lao Tzu described this type of meditation as sitting and letting the mud settle. Often your minds and emotions can be likened to a muddy pool of water. During those times, you can be unclear, turbulent; your light is dim. But if you merely sit and let the mud settle to the bottom of the pond, you can be as clear water, with the sunlight shining through from above.

Another form of meditation is to stand with your arms out in front of you, in a half circle, as if you were hugging someone. With your mind intent, send roots down into the earth at least three times your height. Notice how you stabilize and become rooted in the earth. Stand there for

125

5-20 minutes, drawing healing yin energy up from the earth.

You can even meditate lying down. A famous Taoist master called Chen Tuan, is said to have practiced sleeping meditation for months at a time!

Lie on your right side or on your back. Your palms may be held face up or face down. Concentrate as before, on breathing slowly and deeply, into your lower dan tian, your lower torso. Feel your abdomen expand on the inhale and contract on the exhale. Just continue to lie there, breathing in and out, and imagine that you are receiving healing qi from the universe.

Sometimes in Taoist meditation you can work on gently guiding your qi throughout your meridians or special pathways, such as the *ren mo* which runs up the back of your body, along the spine, and the *du mo*, which runs down the front of your body.

Always remember to gently guide the energy, never forcing it (*wu wei*), allowing it to flow like a stream of water. It is said that qi follows *yi* or the mind. This means that you can guide the qi to where you want it to go merely by using the mind to guide it.

If you have a place of pain or disease breathe the qi into that area by guiding it with your mind, in a gentle and non-forceful manner. Notice the painful area fill up with light and healing.

If you wish to live in harmony with the world you need to be able to live in harmony within yourself. By learning how to sit or stand or lie in meditation, you can become more harmonious and peaceful. Actually, when you practice meditation, you are "doing nothing" in the best Taoist tradition.

As so much emphasis in the West is in "doing" it can seem frivolous or lazy to be not doing. But by "not doing" you can reach areas within yourself that all the "doing" in the world will never be able to reach. You can do less, while accomplishing more.

Meditation is the perfect way to harmonize your inner being with your outer being. By allowing your mind to focus on your breath you can balance both sides of your brain, or your yin and yang natures.

By allowing yourself to "be breathed" you can find that still center in the very midst of an otherwise noisy, clamoring mind that will lead you to true understanding and awareness of your higher or deeper self.

Once you have glimpsed and then experienced this deep inner nature, you will begin to move, in a deeply harmonious manner, into your real life.

Meditation, then, becomes not something that you do for a time to achieve a certain goal but instead is something that you do as a part of living, like breathing itself.

As Lao Tzu says:

Can you hold the body and spirit as one?
Can you avoid their separation?
Concentrating your qi
And becoming pliant,
Can you become like a
Newborn baby?
Clearing your mind and
Contemplating the profound
Can you remain unflawed?
In understanding all things
Can you remain apart from them?
   Chapter 10

This practice is about much more than mere relaxation. It is not only about quieting the mind, (though that is a prerequisite for further practice) but it is also about balancing, strengthening, harmonizing and refining your internal state, in order to be able to delve deeply into the currents of your being to connect to the eternal, ever flowing Tao.

Taoist practice slows and quiets the conscious mind and allows more sense of the universe. While the mind remains in the present through meditation, it supersedes the instability of emotions, the ongoing dialogue of the intellect, and the distractions of the senses. The mind centers on pure consciousness. As the Original Spirit begins to unfold and the innocence of the Embryonic Self reveals its face, Tao begins to radiate throughout your body. Not only do you gain new understandings of yourself, but you become more at one with the universe.

That is the goal of Taoist alchemy; to Return to the Source or Return to Tao. In other words, the goal is to no longer to identify with your limited human self but to be able to experience your unlimited and eternal nature, or Tao.

In this way, you can become one of the self-realized ones, or sages, such as the person Lao Tzu describes in the *Tao Te Ching*.

The sage practices non-action.
She teaches by not speaking,
Achieves all things while
Undertaking nothing,
Creates but does not take credit.
Acts but does not depend
Accomplishes much while not
Claiming merit.
Because she claims no merit
Her work will last forever.
    Chapter 2

To become an Immortal, to become a sage, to become a wise man
or woman, takes the level of commitment not found in the ordinary
person. It is not something you can learn in a weekend workshop or
from reading a book or watching a video.

Teachers can certainly be helpful but it is really your own self-
cultivation that will produce the light that will illuminate your life and
help you to realize your own essential nature as being one with Tao.

This is just what all the internal alchemists were doing. To them the
meaning of "lead" and "gold" meant something else. That something
has been known by many names:

The Philosopher's Stone
Elixir of Immortality
Golden Elixir
Kundalini
Dharmakaya
Golden Flower
Immortal Fetus or Embryo
Embryo of Buddhahood

This idea of an Immortal Embryo goes very far back in Taoist internal
alchemy practice. The basic idea is that through practicing Taoist internal
alchemy, you are able to solidify and transform your internal energetic
state to create a kind of energetic embryo or subtle body that can live
outside your body. Many illustrations can be found in ancient Chinese
texts of the practitioner sitting in meditation with a small fetus floating
above his head.

Taoist nei dan practices are basically a process of refinement.

Essence, breath, and spirit are combined into one entity. Just as the outer alchemists refined their ingredients by mixing and firing them in very specific ways, so also do the inner alchemists mix and fire — through various breathing and meditation techniques — so that they can create something that is even more valuable and precious than gold, the Immortal Embryo.

Then the practitioner runs qi up the back channel or du mo and then down the front channel or ren mo in the small heavenly circuit or microcosmic orbit. By doing these types of body-centered spiritual practices, the practitioner circulates his or her qi to all their limbs and organs, in the macrocosmic orbit. What happens then is that all the qi in the body begins to run very smoothly and strongly.

What this means is that the internal qi or life energy of the body is linked up and running smoothly so that the internal organs can do what they need to do to maintain a healthy and strong system.

The Taoists were able to create both spiritual and physical change in their bodies. By doing energetic practices that were grounded in the body, the Taoists were able to transcend the body, or at least what is the accepted norm for bodies. It is the re-creation of conception, which results in a Golden Embryonic version of yourself.

The famous Taoist alchemist Ke Hung (Ge Hong), 284-364 C.E., advised that physical exercises and sexual yoga only prolong life. Actual immortality and supernatural abilities come from workings of the secret elixir of life. His book, the *Pao-p'u Tzu*, is a treatise on the methods and practices for gaining immortality. It is an interesting combination of both internal and external alchemy, with many complex recipes for attaining not only good health, but the complete reversal of the aging process.

Ge Hong also wrote about three types of Immortals. There are the Immortals who practiced "the deliverance from the corpse" (*shih-chieh*) and, at the moment of death, left their bodies behind but continued to purify until their body disappeared, as in the Rainbow Body stories. There are those who are "earthly immortals" and roam around on sacred mountains.

Four Stages of Meditation

Stage 1: Gathering the light.

比時丹熟更須慈母情嬰兒

氣穴法名無盡藏
歲包於家寂抱空
我問空中誰氏子
僊云是你主人翁

衍准坐卧
龍珠守雖
綿綿若存
念茲在茲

夫婦媾一章
孕蜿蜒之予
悼其情交媾
精泜其氣相
其神陽胎大
小俱得其真

蟠龍今巳化飛龍
聖現神通不可窮
一朝跳出珠光外
渾身直到紫微宮

神水溶液
沆瀣根株
內外無塵
長養聖胎

他日雲飛方見真人朝上帝

Stage 2: Origin of a new being in the place of power.

Stage 3. Separation of the spirit-body for independent existence.

Stage 4: The center in the midst of conditions.

Circulation of the Light: The Microcosmic Orbit

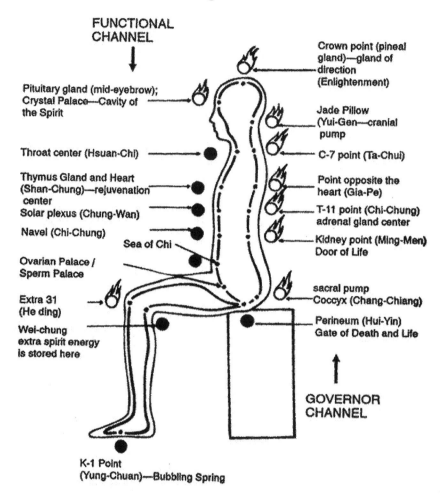

FUNCTIONAL CHANNEL

Pituitary gland (mid-eyebrow); Crystal Palace—Cavity of the Spirit

Throat center (Hsuan-Chi)

Thymus Gland and Heart (Shan-Chung)—rejuvenation center

Solar plexus (Chung-Wan)

Navel (Chi-Chung)

Sea of Chi

Ovarian Palace / Sperm Palace

Extra 31 (He ding)

Wei-chung extra spirit energy is stored here

K-1 Point (Yung-Chuan)—Bubbling Spring

Crown point (pineal gland)—gland of direction (Enlightenment)

Jade Pillow (Yui-Gen—cranial pump

C-7 point (Ta-Chui)

Point opposite the heart (Gia-Pe)

T-11 point (Chi-Chung) adrenal gland center

Kidney point (Ming-Men) Door of Life

sacral pump Coccyx (Chang-Chiang)

Perineum (Hui-Yin) Gate of Death and Life

GOVERNOR CHANNEL

In this practice – called The Circulation of the Light, The Lesser Heavenly Cycle or the Microcosmic Orbit – the practitioner guides chi or light from the perineum point (hui yin) up the back (Du Mai channel) through various energy gates to the top of the head or bai hui point, and then back down the front (Ren Mai channel) all the way to the lower dan tien, in the lower abdomen. In this way various energetic and spiritual centers are opened – providing radiant health, spiritual insight and opening the way to the creation of the Golden Embryo.

Diagram from Mantak and Maneewan Chia Awaken Healing Light of the Tao (Healing Tao Books, 1993), p.170.

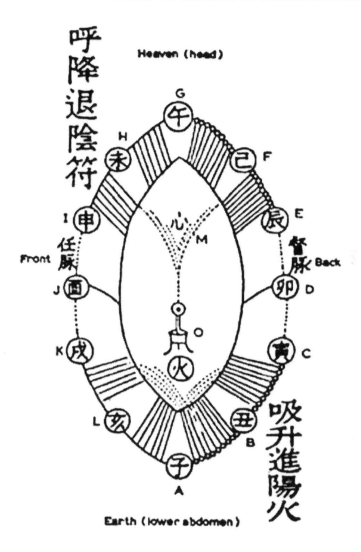

Once the circulation along the Du Mai and Ren Mai is established, this chi energy can be guided through the Chong Mai or central channel, which runs from the perineum or hui yin point to the bai hui point at the top of the head (called Crown Chakra in Indian yoga). This is similar to what in India is called kundalini practice. Then the chi is further refined and transmuted through all three dan tiens – upper (third eye point), middle (heart point) and lower (lower abdomen). Further refinement of the chi can allow the practitioner to create an immortal spirit body or the Golden Embryo.

Image from Taoist Yoga Alchemy & Immortality by Lu K'uan Yu/Charles Luk, Copyright 1973. Used by permission from Red Wheel Book Publishers.

135

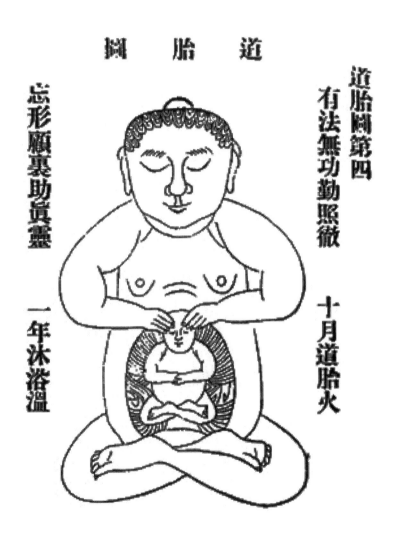

圖　胎　道

道胎圖第四
有法無功勤照徹

十月道胎火

忘形顧裹助眞靈

一年沐浴溫

出 胎 圖

出胎圖第五

身外有身名佛相

千葉蓮花由炁化

念靈無念即菩提

百光景耀假神凝

137

Then there are those who are "heavenly immortals" and "rise up with their bodies and ascend into emptiness."

Regardless of their end result, a practitioner is rewarded at different stages by many things such as improved health, reversal or slowing of the aging process, more balanced emotions, improved intellect, inner clarity etc.

Whether your interest is in immortality, attaining the Immortal Embryo or enlightenment, or just a healthier, more balanced life, Taoist internal alchemy has much to offer. You can have a more youthful appearance and better health, while discovering the true source of yourself.

KEY CONCEPTS
- Essentially, Chinese Alchemy, like the Indian system, works with the experience of spiritual/energetic channels in the human body.
- Practices that allow qi to flow properly will lead toward union with Tao and enlightenment.
- Through practices, one's consciousness is brought back to the point as it existed in the womb, part of a greater, universal consciousness.
- The Three Treasures – *Jing, Qi* and *Shen* – represent the secret of immortality when fully actualized, the Golden Elixir.
- The goal of Chinese alchemy is to create the Immortal Fetus or Golden Embryo. At the time of enlightenment, the meditator achieves an inner vision of a Golden Embryonic version of him or herself.

CHAPTER FIFTEEN
Sacred Union: Sexual Yoga

The Philosopher's Stone was tainted by its link with magic and exotic Eastern spiritual paths. The Holy Roman Catholic Church frowned upon the Asian practices that dared to link human sexuality with higher consciousness.

Joseph Campbell wrote about some of those sexual images found in Tibetan monasteries that offended the sensibilities of Western church leaders:

In the Buddhists lamaseries of Tibet...the holy images and banners show the various Buddhas and Bodhisattvas joined with their Shaktis in embrace, in the yogic posture known as Yab-Yum, "Father-Mother." And the great prayer of the old prayer wheels of Tibet Om Mani Padme Hum, "the jewel (mani) in the lotus (padme),"signifies, on one level: the immanence of nirvana (the jewel) in samsara (the lotus); on another: the arrival of the mind (the jewel) in nirvana (the lotus); but also, as in the icon of the male and female joined: the lingam in the yoni. "Buddhatvam yosidyonisamsritam," states a late Buddhist aphorism: "Buddhahood abides in the female organ."

Joseph Campbell [1]

It was an inevitable sacred union, the union of opposites that creates something new from the interaction of two completely different energies. The *Yab-Yum*, the Tibetan translated version of the Chinese Yin-Yang, is the same combination of female-male, mother-father or heaven-earth. This sacred union is powerful spiritual alchemy.

This conjunction of opposites, joining male and female in sexual yoga, represents the external physical form as well as the internal joining of the inner subtle bodies that results in immortality. Two partners in blissful embrace can create this actual union of inner subtle bodies much more easily than can one person alone. It is difficult for one person to generate enough heat to activate the qi, although that is the goal of heat yoga. Two people create more heat, faster and more easily.

In Western civilization, sexual images invade our media, marketing, advertising, culture, fashion, society and the dizzying crazy quilt of

1 *Oriental Mythology: The Masks of God* by Joseph Campbell, Penguin Books, 1962.

twenty-first century life. So it's no surprise that the average take on tantric sex is to think of it as a method to allow longer periods of sexual intercourse with greater pleasure.

This is not the agenda for true sexual yoga. Male and female sex organs are sacred in other cultures. They not only result in procreation and perpetuation of the species, but also bring enlightenment from the proper conjunction of male and female union. In fact, the oldest theory is that a person can recreate conception within themselves through the practice of sexual yoga and the joining of male and female energies.

In the illustration of Vajrasattva, the yab-yum represents father-mother. It depicts the union of subtle bodies at the time of enlightenment, created by the union of physical bodies. Many followers in Himalayan civilizations achieved enlightenment through these practices. The basic concept is that what happens at the time of human conception is reversed in the enlightenment process. Conception is recreated, resulting in Buddhahood.

This Buddhahood is the reverse of procreation, in which your children bear your grandchildren and grandchildren have your great-grandchildren and so on. It occurs on the subtle body level and actually multiplies the projection and emanation of subtle bodies. To visualize this idea, imagine going to a television studio and being filmed. Your image could then appear on multiple television screens. Similarly, if you achieved the superpower of Buddhahood, your subtle bodies would duplicate and replicate in the same way, but in multiple dimensions. Each version of your body would contain the entire knowledge of your original body and could teach whoever resides in that alternate reality. So in Buddhahood, you have the ability to reach people in each dimension and enable them to achieve enlightenment, the ideal of the Bodhisattva, the ultimate spiritual warrior.

An enlightened person duplicates his subtle bodies universally. By recreating conception in yourself, by seeing your Original Face at the time of enlightenment, you are at one with the universe as well as part of all possible combinations of multiverses.

So in the simple practice of heating the body through sexual yoga, the yab-yum generates enough inner heat to activate the kundalini, which is also the embryo of Buddhahood.

Sexual yoga might be considered the bridge to somewhere, rather than the destination. Sex for pleasure, connection, and communication are all goals for human sexual activity. Reproduction of the human

140

species depends on sexual intercourse.

But this is not the goal of tantric yoga. It focuses on the creative force, transmuting it into higher channels. Tantric sex awakens the kundalini, activates the fusion of the trikaya, and brings enlightenment through a connection of energies.

Vajrasattva in Yab-Yum

Many tantric divinities are represented as being in union with consorts, and these forms are known as 'yab-yum' (father-mother) forms. Their union represents the inseparability of relative and absolute, manifestation and voidness, method and wisdom. They also symbolize the union of what are called the 'solar' and 'lunar' energies, the two poles of subtle energy that flow in the subtle energy system of the human body, which is called the 'Inner Mandala'. When negative and positive circuits are joined in a lighting circuit, a lamp can be lit. When the solar and lunar energies of the subtle energy system of a human being are brought into the state of non-duality, which was their inherent, latent condition from the very beginning, the human being can become illuminated. In the same way that, in the Chinese Taoist system of philosophy, Yin and Yang are seen as two principles of energy that are fundamentally inseparable and mutually interdependent constituents of a totally integrated unity, so, too the solar and lunar energies are seen as fundamentally not-two from the very beginning. Their fundamental unity is symbolized by the Sanskrit syllable 'Evam', which is also a symbol of the 'yab-yum' principle.

Chogyal Namkhai Norbu [2]

Tantra in Sanskrit means *web* or *continuum*. Its roots are in Hinduism as well as Buddhism, with parallels in Taoism. In India, tantra was known as the Chinese Method. Tantra teaches that in partnering male and female principles, creating an alchemical union, we unlock much larger truths and energies, spiritual and otherwise.

Like the breath of life, sex is vital to the continuation of human beings. As a natural euphoriant, sex is vital to humanity's well-being. Unknown to most people, sex is vital to mankind's spiritual elevation.

Stephen T. Chang [3]

Doctor Chang would tell you that in Chinese Medicine, the source of qi is in your reproductive organs. Too much sexual activity depletes your qi. Only when your qi level is balanced and harmonious, will you enjoy the best of health.

What's interesting about both the classical Chinese medicine system and the traditions of tantra is that they fully qualify as scientific attitudes in a Western sense, in that they are systems that have observed phenomena, and they then qualify, quantify and label aspects of the phenomena so that the information and the results of the information can be reproduced. The difference is in perspective, methods and goals.

In fact, if there had been a fusion of the methods of Western science with the methods of Eastern science millennia ago, perhaps both would

2 *The Crystal and the Way of Light: Sutra, Tantra and Dzogchen, Teachings by* Chogyal Namkhai Norbu, Snow Lion Publications, 2000.

3 *The Tao of Sexology* by Stephen T. Chang, Tao Publishing, 1986.

have worked to much better advantage for humankind.

One observation made by the spiritual systems that have used reproductive energy to supercharge the brain is that the same pleasurable stimulation experienced from normal sexuality can occur when the body's qi level is increased. Tantric Buddhists talk about bliss because if qi is activated, it can feel like sexual bliss even without sexual activity.

In fact, in successful meditation a person can have feelings of sexual arousal without sexual imagery. This is successful physiological energetic activation. Qi gong teachers may also refer to the bliss of standing meditation. When qi is activated in a person in a strong trance state, it circulates through the body and generates heat. Using the lower chakras to activate the higher chakras results in experiences of bliss similar to sexual arousal. In fact a totally celibate monk has the possibility of experiencing profound sexual bliss many times greater than other people. He makes the connection between the body's internal energy and greater levels of internal heat and bliss. So when a celibate activates the lower chakra to heat higher chakras, greater heat and qi is generated, which results in higher levels of bliss. It works the same internally whether it is with self-generated yoga techniques, sexual yoga or normal sexual activity. The end result in the highest level is literally a recreation of conception and Buddhahood.

When reproductive energy is used to supercharge the brain, one must proceed with caution. Qi has to be activated methodically and over time with correct methods. The sleeping serpent must be handled carefully or it may strike with devastating intensity.

In Buddhist tantra, sexual yoga can be seen as an avenue of the Middle Way taught by Prince Siddhartha. As so many other seekers of truth, he initially left his comforts and chose the ascetic path in his search. If desire is indeed the cause of dissatisfaction and pain on this wheel of life, then surely denying desire its objectives, and attempting to quench the fire at the roots, will unlock the secrets of life, right? Siddhartha tried it. He even tried to deny his hunger for food. But it didn't work. Moreover, it was after he ate and regained his strength that he meditated under the Bodhi tree and became enlightened.

Many enlightened texts, or *sutras,* have been written about the Middle Way. Surely we can interpret it here as the path that does not deny desires, but sees through their nature. Desires exist. However, the objects of desires should not be our goals, as seekers of spiritual truths. If, however, we can harness the energy of desire in our bodies, link it with mind and spirit, we can then heat the starting point and achieve trikaya. In a way, Siddhartha took the Taoist path to enlightenment. He went with the flow (*wu wei*).

The Chinese characters for *wu-wei* (oo-way) the concept of non-action from Taoism look like this.

When you turn off your ego and function within neutrality or harmony, you find the most effective means to longevity, balance, harmony, and the authentic spirituality that adapts to nature. Water softly flows to fit its situation, over the years it shows its powerful influence as it grinds the rough edges off a stone or cuts a river channel through solid rock.

The prayer of the Kalachakra Path refers to the "dance of the empty body." The idea of emptiness here is very important. As you recall, Buddha had a key experience of the Golden Embryonic version of himself. This occurred while he was deep in meditation. What happened next was that his subtle body leapt and embraced that Golden Embryonic version, which dissolved into the subtle body, which then returned to the physical body. He embraced singularity and became a living Buddha.

"May I be inspired to accomplish the meditations
Of the supreme yogas of the profound tantric path
Of Kalachakra, the king of tantric traditions,
And thus purify and dissolve all physical materiality,
Giving rise to the dance of the empty body
In union with the great unchanging bliss
That in turn induces highest enlightenment,
The state of the primordial Buddha Kalachakra."

From *Prayer of the Kalachakra Path,* by the Sixth Panchen Lama [4]

4 *The Practice of Kalachakra* by Glenn H. Mullin, Snow Lion Publications, 1991.

Thangka by Nick Dudka (www.thangka.ru)

The picture shows Kalachakra as a union of sexual yoga between male and female deities. The purification is so high that he dissolves all physical material, at one with the universe.

How does that happen? The human body is composed of an underlying field of sound. Under that is a field of light and underlying that is a field of space. So matter is a combination of light, sound, and space all vibrating together. A vibration that corresponds to a specific deity can turn the body of substance to a body that is unsubstantial; just like heating water turns it to vapor or cooling it turns it to ice. And so it is that the Rainbow Body represents the human body as frozen light. At the highest level of enlightenment, a person can transform the body from form to emptiness. Every human being has this potential to turn into an enlightened deity by practicing the correct mantra and correct methods through a specific lineage. Tantric theory is based on achieving realization by uniting solar and lunar energy currents within the central channel.

A Tibetan monk in a cave may have a vision or dream of the deity that teaches him. Or he may even visualize himself as that deity. Taking on this superpower, he radically increases his wisdom and strengthens his link to the realm of enlightenment. In the higher enlightened dimensions, he connects to an enlightened being by using the mantra of that being and visualizes himself as transforming to that deity. This practice allows him to transform to the enlightened being, which we all have within us. Monks learn the correct techniques from masters from specific lineages.

So in the illustration of Kalachakra, you see a visualization that rises from emptiness and dissolves into emptiness, the ground of all being. Form is all emptiness and emptiness is all form. Zero creates one; zero is higher than one. At the highest level of spiritual awakening, you see your Original Face dissolve into emptiness. You become nothing and everything.

Tantra uses sexual attraction in a reflective manner, to harness this energy in order to achieve a higher purpose. The ideas of tantra and alchemy practiced in their original versions were likely the root sources for Eastern awakenings. Tantra works with energy as it exists in the body and with proper teaching can be a swift route to full spiritual awakening.

This quote from the *Cittavisuddhiprakarana* seminal text reminds us that the reproductive energy of the body can be used to transform you to a divine being, which is who you really are. All of life can be used to enhance spiritual practice and turn you into a highly evolved spiritual being.

Desire, enjoyed by the ignorant,
becomes Bondage.
That very same desire,
tasted by one with understanding
brings liberation. [5]

In Tantric theory even self-destructive elements can be transformed from poison to healing elixir if handled with proper knowledge. There are techniques that allow you to realize that the world is enlightened and that you have always been an enlightened being. You can connect yourself while in your body with the world of the enlightened. All experiences are meant to transform you to the enlightened being that you already are.

You can shed all illusions and recognize the truth. Your body is a microcosm of the universe. You are complete. When you unite your mind and body, you may discover your true self. This is done by cultivating your qi, because this is the connecting point of universal energy. All these techniques of meditation, tai chi, qi gong, and yoga cultivate the connection between your body and mind with the universal mind.

In her book, *Passionate Enlightenment*, Miranda Shaw explains how unique Tantric Buddhism is among the Buddhist sub-traditions. Tantra honors the body and recognizes the power within the body as a source of knowledge. This "abode of bliss" allows the energy of desire, sexuality and pleasure to be used to help a person to move along the pathway to enlightenment. Founders of the tantric movement discovered and developed cooperative sexual yoga techniques that allow the relationships between men and women to be used for self liberation, for awakening the spirit.

Tibetan ritual chants also use two objects – the *dorje*, called the Diamond Thunderbolt Scepter, is the male – a phallic symbol that represents compassion. The bell is the female and represents wisdom. Manipulated together during the ritual, these two objects dance together in a cosmic dance of male and female, compassion and wisdom.

The thunderbolt is the image of power in nature. It represents the ultimate power in divinity. When thunder rumbles and lightning cracks

5 *The Cittavisuddhiprakarana*: http://www.exoticindiaart.com/book/details/IDK434/

with a sudden flash of light, we are reminded of the brightness of the moment when we see our Original Face or when our kundalini is activated. The breakthrough of a spiritual leap or experience that fires the brain.

In this way the rituals represent subtle body activation and subtle body union.

The Bell and Dorje

Symbolically a dorje represents the 'thunderbolt of enlightenment,' that abrupt change in human consciousness which is recognized by all the great religions as a pivotal episode in the lives of mystics and saints. The bell and dorje, or thunderbolt, are inseparable ritual objects in Tibetan Buddhism. They are always used in combination during religious ceremonies. The bell held in the left hand, represents the female aspect as wisdom; the dorje, or male is held in the right hand, representing wisdom. Together, they represent the union of wisdom and method, or the attainment of Enlightenment.

In *Vajrayana*, or Thunderbolt Vehicle Practice, it is taught that after reaching enlightenment the Buddha returned to his palace and reunited with his wife. Some sources even claim the Buddha achieved enlightenment through sexual yoga practice before leaving the palace.

At the level of Thunderbolt Buddhism, sexual identity assumes symbolic significance, and sexual communion assumes sacramental status.[6]

In these schools of Buddhist practice, trying to reach enlightenment without tantric union is likened to using water to churn butter. It is the same as saying there can be no enlightenment without sexual yoga.

In the seventh century text called the *Cittavisuddhiprakarana* we find the following passage in which the lotus symbolizes the vagina and the vajra, or thunderbolt, symbolizes the penis as they reach a circular cosmic unity:

> That blissful delight that consists between lotus
> and vajra,
> Who does not rejoice there?
> This moment may be the bliss of means,
> or of both wisdom and means.
> It is profound, it is vast.
> It is neither self nor other.
> Even as the moon makes light in black darkness,
> So in one moment the supreme bliss removes all defilement.
> When the sun of suffering has set,
> Then arises this bliss, this lord of the stars.
> It creates with continuous creativity,
> And of this comes the mandala circle.
> Gain purification in bliss supreme,
> For here lies final perfection.

To truly understand this philosophy and to be able to do these practices it is of utmost importance to be able to study the texts quoted from and, most importantly, to find a teacher, a lama. It is said that the tantric path can be a slippery slope without proper understanding and guidance. Without correct preparation, self-cultivation, and deep understanding of the principles involved, one will only be indulging in low level desires and not truly walking the tantric path.

The main point here is to introduce the idea that sexuality can be viewed as well as experienced by the spiritual seeker as an important and integral part of the path.

At the same time tantric exercises were being developed in India,

6 *Twilight Goddess by* Thomas Cleary & Sartaz Aziz, *Shambhala Publications, 2000.*

similar work was happening in China. Sexual yoga involving male/female couples is traditionally one of the main branches of internal alchemy (*nei dan*) in China. The always practical Taoists proposed using what was readily accessible, the energy of sexual attraction. Wise Taoists of old practiced a kind of tantric sex with wives and concubines. These Taoists believed that their male energy, which was built up during these sessions, had far better uses than to be ejaculated into the female during intercourse.

In fact, the idea was to conserve their jing, their sexual energy, by refraining from ejaculation. Thus the energy produced from this alchemical wedding of yin and yang could be directed through the body/mind/spirit channels, not just for spiritual enlightenment, but for radiant health and longevity.

Eastern scholars found the original source of sexual yoga techniques to have come from the Yellow Emperor. It is written that he was visited one night by three Immortal Maidens and instructed in the Art of the Bedchamber.

The poor Emperor was worn out with trying to satisfy his hundreds of concubines. Sleep deprived and physically depleted, the Emperor, Huang Ti, looked at the Lady Immortals with hollow eyes. They knew he was in dire need of their assistance.

"I am exhausted and in disharmony. I am sad and worry constantly. I fear that I am not up to the task of Emperor if I cannot perform my duties as the Royal Husband," he cried, wringing his hands in despair.

He paced the floor. Then stopped and shook his head with frustration and with all the misery a distraught emperor could show he finally asked, "What shall I do about this?"

Su Nu, the Plain Maiden, took pity upon the exhausted man who stood abjectly in front of her, looking for any help and not expecting any. She told him that all his problems were from faulty ways of loving. She advised him that women were stronger in sex than men. Those who do not know the true Way of Loving would die before their time. In addition, they would die without enjoying the pleasures of living.

At first, Huang Ti did not want to believe this. Long nights of little sleep and sexual activity with his multiple wives had exhausted him beyond thinking of having sex again. He despaired of any more sexual activity. He was completely worn out.

But he was only chastised for his attitude. Then he was told about yin and yang and of their activities and changes and how important it was for humans to not do anything against the flow of nature. He heard that yin and yang must be in clear communication in order to harmonize with each other.

Trying to understand but still unconvinced he asked the Lady Immortals, "How then, can I continue to have relations with so many women and not exhaust myself, but be in harmony with them?"

The three maidens then instructed him in the secret arts of the bedchamber. He was told how to make love and control his emissions. They called this "the return of the jing", which they assured was very beneficial to a man's health.

Samantabadhra

According to the Tibetan Nyingma tradition, the Vajrayana Samantabhadra (Tibetan: kun tu zang po) is a primordial (Adi) buddha. With his naked deep blue body in union with his white consort, he represents the symbol of dharmakaya and is of central significance.

The Emperor then began to understand and regained his good disposition. He spent several nights in close company with the Simple Maid, the Mysterious Maid and the Chosen Maid. During that time, they taught him everything he needed to know about ideas and techniques to make love while staying in harmony with nature. The lessons he learned became known as the Art of the Bedchamber.

The arts were written in a secret way so as not to be available to the merely curious. They are in fact a combination of meditation, qi gong, visualization and breath work. As with all Taoist practices, there must be balance, harmony, and naturalness. This practice involves surrender, trust and self-discipline as opposed to self-denial.

To put it extremely simply – in Chinese sexual practice, woman is considered the energetic superior to man and it is the role of the man to serve the woman. It is believed that if a man induces a great amount of sexual energy by lovemaking and is able to withhold his ejaculation and instead bring that energy up his *du mai* channel (along the spine) to the head, then this energy will transform to pure spiritual elixir.

In Taoist sexual practice woman is seen as water, slow to boil, while man is seen as fire, all too quickly coming to a boil and then flaming out. Thus in Taoist lovemaking the man learns to pace himself to the woman. For once the water of the woman comes to a boil she can sustain her peak energy for much longer than most men. Taoism holds great veneration for woman and for the yin principle in particular. Lao Tzu tells us to "know the yang but hold to the yin."

Sexuality, the joining of all natural forces in the rhythm of yin and yang, is at the center of the Daoist universe. It appears either as codified marital relations and formal sexual rites or, in the case of celibate practitioners, as an imaginary union with a divine partner. [7]

In Taoist thought, women are said to be naturally closer to Tao and thus can move much faster on the spiritual path.

Ge Hong, one of the most famous Taoist alchemists, taught that without knowing how to balance, harmonize, and control sexual energy, a person could not attain enlightenment. Taking ginseng or magic elixirs would not be enough. And although managing the Three Treasures (jing, qi and shen) is essential, any balancing work done for the purpose of increasing longevity would be to no avail if a man ejaculated with a concubine every night. Qi cultivation is not successful if it is wasted in sexual activity. In Chinese medicine, excessive male masturbation is thought to damage health, weaken the spine, and take years off life. Excess

7 *Women in Daoism* by Catherine Despeux, Daoism Handbook, Brill, 2000.

of any kind is damaging. Also any extremes of emotion for long periods of time is considered to be damaging to internal organs. A person who is angry all the time could damage their liver, for instance. Balance is the goal.

When your body is out of balance, it suffers some form of stress. Modern Western medicine recognizes the detrimental effect to health from prolonged periods of stress. Stress increases cholesterol, glucose, triglycerides, cortisol, blood pressure and pain. It decreases serotonin and dopamine, neurotransmitters needed to avoid depression. It disrupts sleep and decreases the immune function. Stress affects memory and decreases sexual desire and performance. So keeping your body in balance is a healthy goal.

The Chinese had seen that people who lived long lives did so by keeping all things in balance. Military and government leaders died young when they were oversexed or killed others. They were killed in return or weakened by excessive appetites. Overeating or overindulgence of any kind led to illness. Elixirs taken in excess could poison a person, just as a drug overdose can kill from too much of an otherwise helpful prescription drug. By remaining in harmony, staying in balance, illnesses could be avoided. Regulating eating, breathing, and exercise in relation to the season and harmonizing the qi to maintain balance were seen as practical measures to maintain good health and well-being.

Avoiding the attention of people in control was a method that kept one safe from early death. You would be less likely to end up in jail or executed by keeping a low profile. Regimes change and destroy those that preceded them. Spiritual masters did not draw attention to themselves. They were wise not to seek out power or acclaim for themselves.

In the Taoist tradition it was considered wise to live in harmony with the patterns found in nature. Women were particularly venerated because they were seen to be more in harmony with nature, closer to the primordial powers of the cosmos. And clearly the woman's sexuality was stronger than a man's. Power and energy were found in the vagina and there wasn't a loss of qi from female orgasms. The male who ejaculated frequently lost physical health and longevity as well as being unable to reach enlightenment. The man who recognized the sexual superiority of woman had an understanding that would be to his advantage. When taught proper skills, he could benefit from the woman's sexual energy, by heating up his starting point, activating his kundalini, increasing his qi, growing spiritually and deepening his spiritual awareness.

It is in taking control of his emissions that the man is able to not only match the energy of the woman but he is also able to save his *jing* and use that energy for greater health as well as spiritual cultivation.

Of course for this to work it involves slowing down and becoming sensitive to each other's energy. It also involves a certain kind of surrender on the man's part. The man must learn to curtail a certain amount of his pleasure, not only to serve the woman but also to be able to transform his sexual energy into pure qi and then to shen or spiritual energy. The Chinese developed a highly sophisticated system of using the energy or qi of the body in order to actually transcend the body itself.

Taoists are eminently practical. They developed a way to use sex as a tool and a practice for longevity, illumination, self-awareness, energy exchange, and personal health. All for the same price!

By using the Tao of Sex a man and woman can arrive at the place that Grand Master Mantak Chia so eloquently describes:

When the exchange of *ching chi* (sexual energy) reaches a certain intensity and balance, the solid bodies of the two lovers begin pulsating as if charged with electricity. The feeling of having solid flesh disappears. You are suddenly a pillar of vibrating energy held in exquisite balance by your lover's field of energy. This is a total orgasm of body and soul. The battling ego shrinks to the true size, a tiny grain of sand, and reluctantly begins humming in chorus with the ocean of the subtle universe that rhythmically washes over it. [8]

The Taoist way is not to go against nature, but to use all aspects of life for one's self-cultivation. Taoist practice is much more than just meditation or qi gong practice. Instead, it is a way to use every aspect of one's life to further one's spiritual goals. To be able to use the powerful and often dangerous energy of sexuality to further one's spiritual cultivation is a high level practice indeed, when taught correctly by a master of a true lineage.

There is no mahamudra without karmamudra.
(There is no enlightenment without sexual yoga.)
...famous Tibetan tantric saying

Again, the Taoists are saying that by using the energy or qi of the

8 *Taoist Secrets of Love: Cultivating Male Sexual Energy* by Mantak Chia and Michael Winn, Aurora Press, 1984.

body one can not only benefit one's health but bring one closer to what is known in Taoism as Returning to the Source. And, instead of banning sex altogether as do many other spiritual paths, Taoism instead uses this powerful energy to open energetic and spiritual centers in the body so that they can become filled with qi, light, and deep awareness and understanding.

KEY CONCEPTS
- Tantra is a discipline to harness inner powers toward spiritual purposes beyond the realms of culture, society and ego. There are Hindu, Buddhist and Jain versions of tantra.
- Tantra can be practiced alone, through meditation and yoga, as well as with a partner.
- Tantra has counterparts in other systems, including Chinese Taoism.
- There are many systems in China, India and Tibet which emphasize sexual yoga as one of the most ancient and complete methods for achieving enlightenment as well as health and longevity.

CHAPTER SIXTEEN
Chinese Medicine

For thousands of years, a practical system of medicine has been in use in China. It's a system that has the potential to change the entire model of our Western healthcare system and how we view sickness, disease and healing. One component of this system, acupuncture, is already used in many health programs in the West and has proved successful in treating many ailments, including pain management. It has gained status within the alternative therapeutic fields and has been recognized by many health insurance programs. Since 1989, a standard for acupuncture licensure has been in place in many states. This ancient system began as classical Chinese Medicine, with roots going back to the days when shamans doctored their community.

Long, long ago, in the early years of the Sui Dynasty, there was a medicine sage called Sun Simiao (581-682 CE). Even as a child, he was fascinated with healing herbs and their medicinal qualities. By age twelve he knew many of them by name and how to use them. By the time he was sixteen, his skill in diagnostics and prescribing herbs was said to surpass that of doctors with much more experience. His expertise in increasing longevity was well known, for which purpose he brewed certain herbs that helped to preserve and circulate qi, the internal energy that is most essential for good health.

One morning, Sun Simiao was collecting herbs by the river. He saw a bright green squiggle in the tall grass and stopped what he was doing to take a closer look. Kneeling down, he saw it was a small green snake with a large gash along its side. Sun Simiao took a jar of healing ointment from his bag and gently applied it along the little snake's limp body. He then took a packet of herbs from his bag, crushed them in the palm of his hand, and added drops of clear water from the river until he was satisfied that the paste was just right for the snake. He put his palm under its head, watching as the little snake flicked its tongue out and tasted the herbs. Patiently he crouched beside the little snake, watching until it had eaten all of the herbal paste. Then he stood back. The snake lifted its tiny head in acknowledgement and slithered out of sight through the tall grass.

The following week, Sun Simiao was gathering herbs again at the same river when he looked up and saw an old man in red and gold robes and a small child dressed in green walking toward him. As they neared him they revealed their true identities as snake spirits and guardians of the river. This grandfather and grandson thanked Simiao for his life-saving work and invited him to their home. When Simiao followed them into the river, he found himself magically transported into a beautiful mansion with tables of delectable fish of many kinds.

Simiao immediately apologized for not partaking of the fine meal, explaining that he could not eat any sentient beings. The old man wanted to give him something to show their gratitude and realizing Simiao would accept no payment, presented him with a catalog of herbs that grew specifically on riverbanks along with a manual on how to use the herbs.

Simiao was delighted with the gifts, knowing that now he could help even more people and animals. He earnestly studied the writings and set forth, using the new information to successfully treat many incurable diseases.

His reputation soon reached the royal court and the emperor asked him to come to the palace to be the official royal physician. But Sun Simiao knew the emperor's reputation and believed that he did not rule in the best interests of his people and that his interest was selfishly focused on an elixir of immortality for himself. So Sun Simiao declined, saying he would serve better by completing a master catalog of herbs. And indeed, the emperor and his dynasty did not last long after because the people rebelled against his harsh treatment.

Tang Taizong replaced the corrupt regime and soon began a golden age for China, the Tang Dynasty (618-907 CE). He lowered taxes and fed the poor from his own granaries and supported an open trade with Japan, Tibet, India, and Persia. China and its people prospered. Again, Sun Simiao was invited to join the court as the royal physician. Again he declined, but offered to advise on medical matters as needed.

When Sun Simiao answered Taizong's formal invitation to court, they discussed longevity. The emperor was interested in Simiao's simple lifestyle and healing through stillness. However, he felt it was not the lifestyle for a ruler, with a primary duty to his people.

Sun Simiao continued documenting his knowledge and healing with medicinal herbs and died peacefully at the esteemed age of ninety. Just after his last breath, observers saw a mist fill the room, coil around his lifeless body, and lift Simiao's spirit body up and away in the grasp of two intertwining snakes. (Two coiling snakes can be seen today as symbols of Western medicine.)

This story is most important, however, for its representation of the shamanic ability to communicate with animals and spirits as well as the tradition of a mythical manual that is found and passed on from teacher to student.

The first known such book in Chinese medicine, which still exists today, is the *Neijing* or *Classic of Internal Medicine* by Huangdi, also known as the Yellow Emperor. It was written two hundred years before the birth of Christ. In truth, the *Neijing* is a source of medical material based on a collection of practices that went on long before it was written. This is the same Yellow Emperor who taught arts of longevity and immortality, mastering the energies of the body through sexual yoga practices, and achieving enlightenment as a sage king.

Chivalry and self-sacrifice were always part of the model of Chinese medicine. In all the ancient stories, a person of virtue or an Immortal mirrored the world of the enlightened, for wisdom is the province of the virtuous. The Mandate of Heaven is given until it becomes corrupted. The healer is motivated to save lives and passes down their knowledge through the ages to worthy students whose desire is to benefit their people.

Many more texts followed over the years, based on experiment as well as on knowledge and experience accrued in a long tradition of healers. Originally, classical Chinese Medicine had many branches, including acupuncture, qi exercises (*dao yin*), meditation, massage (*anmo*), herbology, astrology, and *feng shui* (geomancy). However, when the People's Republic of China was founded, many of these branches were dropped, and disdained as relics of "feudal" times. Variations of massage, acupuncture and herbology were kept, creating what is today known as Traditional Chinese Medicine (TCM). Many strands of classical Chinese Medicine were codified and standardized, with most of the shamanic, or nature related parts, removed.

The magical elements of shamanism and alchemy were linked. Alchemy was the oldest art in China and although alchemists may have died from mercury poisoning — from the mixing of gold ore with mercury and heating and reheating them in an attempt to extract pure gold — the real treasure was found with the Golden Embryo, the Original Face of enlightenment. There were also techniques of medical sexual alchemy said to result in immortality. There were even branches of Chinese medicine that dealt with exorcisms and finding ghost points to remove hauntings or demonic attacks. There were possession versions and branches that emphasized mediumship or channeling with automatic writing. The Chinese doctor was an alchemist, an exorcist, and a shaman who worked on the cultivation of the Three Treasures to create immortals, sages, or enlightened people. This was the core knowledge underlying Chinese Medicine. Recently there has been a rediscovery of Classical Acupuncture or Five Element Acupuncture. Classical acupuncture had become illegal to practice in China so it subsequently went underground, to be found again by the exploratory minds of the West.

In fact, Classical Chinese Medicine was in danger of being dropped completely in the Communist's quest for modernization and letting go of ancient traditions. Except for one fact, it may well have been lost completely; it was found useful on what is known as the Long March. Thousands of soldiers in the Communist Red Army retreated from the Chinese Nationalist troops during the Chinese Civil War. Only one tenth of those who started survived the year-long circular retreat over the most difficult terrain in China. Traditional healers along on the march saved thousands of men during the epic trek across China. Their effectiveness could not be ignored.

As a matter of fact, once the Communists controlled all of China, Mao instituted a movement called Barefoot Doctors. With inadequate numbers of trained doctors to treat the huge population, and most of them working in cities, some eighty percent of the rural population had no access to medical care. Thousands of young peasant women and men were selected from their villages and sent for intensive medical training in hospitals. They studied anatomy, bacteriology, diagnostics, birth control, prenatal and infant care, acupuncture and both Chinese herbal medicine and Western medicine. Then they returned to their communities where they helped as primary care health providers — giving immunizations, delivering babies, and overseeing vast sanitation improvements.

This integrated medicine, a combination of East and West, is known now as Traditional Chinese Medicine or TCM. It is still a very powerful form of medicine and is used by millions of people in Asia as well as in the West.

Modern medicine in the West has certainly made great strides in the world of technology and infectious diseases, introducing x-ray machines, computed tomography, and vaccines, for instance. But Traditional Chinese Medicine often works more successfully for chronic diseases such as chronic fatigue syndrome, multiple sclerosis, and fibromyalgia.

Acupuncture uses the basic energy of the body, qi, whose motion and energy transformation is basic to life. Qi moves up and down meridians and transforms within the body. The unity of body with emotional and mental activities is essential for good health. When yin and yang are not in balance in the body, disease can manifest, whereas a good balance of yin/yang will thwart disease. It is all interconnected; it is one organic whole that responds to the forces of yin/yang and the movement of qi within the body.

Strong emotions, obsessive thoughts, or physical, emotional or spiritual traumas upset the balance and flow of qi. It is taught in Chinese medicine that certain emotions are related to specific organ systems. For instance, it is taught that anger resides in the liver, causing liver imbalances. Happiness and joy is related to the health of the heart meridian. Worry affects the spleen. Grief is felt in the lungs. Fear impacts kidney health.

Similarly, in Western medicine, stress affects the circulatory system, immune system, endocrine and nervous systems. Stress is related to weight gain and increases pain. It is widely held as a risk factor in many diseases. The importance of a healthy union of body, mind, and emotions is documented in both cultures.

Chinese Medicine uses the premise that processes of the human body are interrelated and in constant interaction with the environment. Signs of disharmony help the practitioner to understand, treat and prevent illness and disease. The concepts of yin/yang, the Five Phases (wu hsing), and meridians of the body are central to diagnosis and treatment.

The scientific model in Chinese medicine is to harmonize, balance, and increase the good qi within the meridians, decrease the bad qi, and clear the blockages. Many illnesses are caused by disrupted flow in qi caused by a disturbed physical, mental or spiritual state. Once the blockage is removed and the energy is balanced, the body is capable of healing itself and will do so. To be healthy qi must flow steadily and harmoniously.

Western medicine has also begun to embrace the concept of integrative medicine and the value of incorporating the methods that come from embracing a paradigm for good health that is based on the unity of mind and body. More and more doctors, physician's assistants, and nurse practitioners promote nutrition and exercise as well as the benefits of incorporating techniques of yoga, tai chi, meditation, and qi gong into a health regimen. Many doctors have witnessed miracles of healing due to the effect of prayer or positive thinking. Often doctors intentionally give their patients a sense of hope, to allow the natural mind–body healing connection to work its magic.

Chinese medicine would recognize this as the mind and spirit transforming the body through the internal meridian pathways. The integration of acupuncture and Chinese medicine with Western Medicine not only augments, but actually transforms the paradigm of Western medical science. The new paradigm not only focuses on healing, curing illnesses, and promoting long life, but potentially, it will create the launching point for the evolution of collective human consciousness.

Chinese Medicine is considered a more holistic approach than modern Western medicine. It involves a multi-dimensional paradigm. Chinese Medicine essentially honors the three bodies; the physical body, the subtle body, and the super-subtle body. Or, if you prefer, it works with not just the body, but the mind and the spirit. It sees the human body as a microcosm for all of Nature. Observing Nature outside and how it works, it attempts to use Nature as it works within the body for healing and transformation.

Chinese Medicine works from Nature backward. In other words, it sees enlightened Nature itself as a model or paradigm. The macrocosm is a conscious living and breathing Universe, evident to us in Nature itself. Our bodies are the microcosm of that living, breathing conscious universe.

Observing that our bodies are not in this ideal state, acupuncturists use qi, the natural energy of the body, to help put them back in balance. Enlightenment is the model. Good health is the goal. A person who gets acupuncture treatments or sees a Chinese herbalist won't necessarily achieve Buddhahood, or realization of Tao, but they will be moved to a more balanced state where the potential to recognize their true nature will increase.

Dr. Mary Loo, MD, Clinical Assistant Professor at Stanford Medical Center and author of *East-West Healing* (about the integration of Eastern and Western medical systems),[1] has an interesting observation on the future of qi. She is confident that, in the near future, technology will be able to identify and measure qi, the bioenergetic basis of Chinese medicine. She said, "It's already been determined, for example, that qi has electromagnetic properties. Qi is also starting to be described

1 *East-West Healing* by Mary Loo, John Wiley and Son 2001.

161

as the wave or energy part of the human body, while the anatomical-biochemical model is the particle or matter part."

Chinese Medicine has established over the centuries that qi is everywhere in the body. It circulates in the body along channels, called meridians. As part of the blood, it moves within blood vessels. As part of organs and tissues, it functions within them. It is the foundation of our being, the starting point of our body. Qi is primordial and androgynous, the bonding of yin and yang, there at conception, connecting us to the conscious universe. It is the portal through which we become the conscious universe.

Spirit and consciousness are primal. They are expressed because they are inherent in our bodies. Consciousness exists in spirit, or *shen*. From this great primal universal field of consciousness in spirit, miracles of healing are made.

The Gospels of Matthew, Mark, Luke, and John all tell stories of healing miracles performed by Jesus Christ. He healed leprosy, epilepsy, deafness and mutism, blindness, paralyzed limbs, shriveled bodies, and the deathly ill. He healed through the spirit.

Chinese Medicine says that spirit flows through us in a directional pathway, along the channels and meridians. When qi is flowing smoothly, when the body is in harmony with Nature – the microcosm linked with the macrocosm – then the body is healthy. However, when the qi does not flow properly, then the goal of Chinese Medicine is, through acupuncture, acupressure and other systems, to diagnose the points of blockage and deficiency, remove the blockage and increase qi, so that meridians can flow naturally.

There is a resemblance between these channels and the channels in the chakra system. Interestingly enough, pre-modern Western medicine had a more primitive notion of "flows." Surgeons and barbers would make small cuts in sick patients to "let blood." Leeches were used to tap out bad elements and "thin" blood. As recently as The Age of Reason in the Eighteenth Century, people spoke about the *humors* flowing through the body. Educated, refined women in bad moods were said to have a case of the *vapors*. Western herbal remedies, have of course, always been used, all dating back to man's shamanic bond with Nature.

Much in the manner chemistry can be traced back to Western alchemy, so Chinese Medicine can be traced back to Chinese alchemy.

This is a very ancient system. In Five Phases or Five Element Theory, there is a link between the human body, mind and spirit, and nature through Five Elements — Water, Wood, Fire, Earth and Metal (Gold in the ancient alchemical texts). There's an ancient alchemical saying, "reverse the cycle of the five elements and the dragon appears in the fire." It means that if you reverse the whole embryonic development process, you create the Spiritual Embryo, which is the dragon appearing in the fire. Chinese medical alchemy works with the concept of reversing the developmental stages of the body's energy to recreate conception and enable you to transcend birth, death, space, and time.

The human body has a seamless interrelationship with Nature. Just as in Nature, in the human body these elements must be in balance. A doctor's goal in the Classical or Five Element System is to balance these elements within the physical body. There are meridians that correspond to body organs. Water corresponds with the kidneys and bladder meridians. Wood corresponds with the liver and gall bladder meridians. Fire corresponds with the heart and small intestines. Earth corresponds with the spleen, pancreas and stomach. Metal (Gold) corresponds with the lungs and colon.

In what is called the creation cycle each season of the year flows into the next with its respective element. It begins with the winds blowing from the heavens. These winds thus create Wood or Spring. Wood becomes fuel for the fiery season of Summer. The fire of Summer produces ashes, which become the soil of Late Summer, or the bounty of Earth. Earth condenses and is hardened and purified, creating the metal or gold of Autumn. And metal becomes a container of the primordial waters of Winter. In the old medical texts the Five Phases are illustrated as a circle with Earth in the center.

The Five Elements or Phases are used extensively in classical or Five Element Acupuncture to treat a wide variety of health issues but they are also used in nei dan or internal alchemy practices. In Chinese thought, everything in the universe is connected in various ways of support as well as control. For instance, when treating a patient for a problem in the lungs, the doctor (*dai fu*) may treat the lungs or they may treat the element just before the lungs, the Earth element. This is called "treating the mother to cure the child." In this way, the practitioner is able to treat the causative factor, or the factor arising in the patient's nature that is not in harmony with the whole. By treating the "mother element," the "child element" will be appeased and will stop crying out in the form of a symptom. It is understood that the human body is not a machine, so isolating parts from other parts instead of treating the whole system, will

163

not be conducive to healing.

This idea that everything exists only in relation to everything else is the major key to understanding Taoist internal alchemy, whether it is medicine, art, or spiritual practice.

In Lao Tzu's work, the *Tao Te Ching*, we find the following supporting passage:

Under heaven everyone knows that the existence of beauty
Depends on the existence of ugliness.
Everyone knows the capacity of kindness
Depends on the existence of the unkind.
Existence and nothingness are mutually born,
Difficult and easy complete each other,
Long and short shape each other,
Tall and short rest upon each other,
Sound and music harmonize each other,
Before and after follow one another.
Chapter 2

Wu Xing (Five Elements)

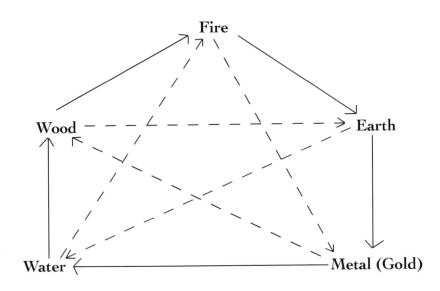

Interactions of Five Chinese Elements - Cycles of Balance and Cycles of Imbalance

164

Here's an organ balancing meditation exercise you can do with the five elements from Solala Towler's book *Embarking on the Way: A Guide to Western Taoism:*

You may start by either sitting or lying down quietly, breathing gently and slowly, from the belly, eyes closed, seeing with your mind's eye.

Imagine a cloud of light hovering just above your head. It can be a billowy, fluffy cloud, or a sparkling cloud of energy, or whatever other form feels right to you. Feel it floating there, just above your head, for a moment or two. Then let it slowly sink down through the top of your head, through your crown, to settle in your heart.

Here it becomes a bright, vibrant red. Red is the color of summer, when all of life is at its peak. It is a joyous, creative time, when the bright sun shines mightily down upon us all. Feel this season in your heart as the red cloud pulses slowly in your chest. The element is Fire, the fire of controlled passion and creativity.

The heart's job is to keep the blood moving freely throughout the body. It is also the home of the shen, or spirit. It is that which makes us human, that which gives us consciousness.

The negative emotion connected with the heart is hysteria. The positive, which we are emphasizing right now, is joy and creativity. So picture this vibrant red cloud lying lightly on your heart, filling it with joy and purpose, openness and creativity.

Sit and relax for a little bit and allow yourself to feel this deep within you. Remember, in Taoist practice, "qi follows yi," or energy goes with the mind. Wherever you put your attention is where the energy will go, positively or negatively. This is why it is important to always keep our thoughts positive and supportive so this will be the kind of energy we will not only attract, but create within ourselves.

Next move down to the left side of your abdomen to your spleen/ stomach area. Here the cloud turns to a deep, earthy yellow. The spleen element is Earth, its season is harvest time or, as was observed in ancient times, the pause between seasons. It is the grounding force in our being.

The spleen helps our digestion, extracting the qi from what we eat. It also helps us digest our experiences. The negative emotion connected to the spleen is worry or self-absorption. The positive emotion is empathy.

Take a little time here and allow yourself to feel your empathy and connection to the earth and to all living things. Feel the groundedness

165

of your being. Sink your roots deep into the earth; draw up the pure yin qi found there and let it fill you up, from the bottom of your feet to the top of your head.

Now move the cloud up to your chest and into your lungs. When it reaches your lungs it turns bright white. It hovers there, within your lungs, filling them with vital, healing energy. The corresponding season is autumn, the time when growing things are beginning to close up shop for the long sleep of winter. The element is Metal or Gold.

The lungs rule the respiration, our ability to extract oxygen and other nutrients, as well as qi, from the air around us. And they govern our *wei* or protective qi, guarding us against outside evils or attacking forces like colds and flu. Picture then, your lungs becoming strong and healthy, expanding easily with each breath, sending out the protective qi to all parts of your body, each cell expanding and contracting as you breathe deeply through your belly.

The negative emotion connected with the lungs is grief. It is here we feel our sadness, our loss. And while we acknowledge the importance of connecting to that grief and not denying or suppressing it, at this time we would like to emphasize the positive emotions of courage and the ability to surrender deeply to each moment.

We picture and feel these attributes of courage and the ability to surrender as we see this bright white cloud of energy lying loosely upon our lungs.

Next we move to our lower back, to the kidneys. Here the cloud turns a deep blue/black, almost black. The element is Water, the season winter, the time when earth energy is dormant and deep. The kidney/adrenal area is the seat of our will. It also is the source of our day-to-day energy, the pilot light beneath our furnace.

Here we store our sense of will and determination, our "backbone." The negative emotion associated with the kidneys is fear. The kidneys are a strong part of our "root" system; here we experience the fear and anxiety in our lives. But now we will instill willpower and the ability to deal with our lives in a positive and creative fashion.

At this point we can sit for a few moments and allow ourselves to breathe deeply into our kidneys, located in our lower back. Each breath fills them with powerful qi so they will be able to hold us up, both in our daily lives and in all our endeavors. Our kidneys are where we store our prenatal qi or jing, which is very important to our physical and mental development. It is also the repository of our generative or sexual energy.

166

Because the very pulse of life starts here, it is important that we work on creating strong kidney energy and not dissipate it through a self-abusive lifestyle.

From here the cloud moves up to the right side of the body, just below and underneath the rib cage, to the liver. Here it becomes a rich green, the green of spring, of new growth, of expansion and free-flowingness. The element is Wood, the wood of plants, grasses and trees. It is the season of spring, of new beginnings, and of outward expansion.

The liver, besides acting as a filter for the toxins in our system, regulates movement within the body. The ability for blood, qi and even emotions to move freely through the system is governed by our liver.

As we meditate, we picture our liver as being a rich green, supple and flexible, better able to help us move through the changes in our lives. We picture ourselves as the rich new growth of spring, resilient, strong and supple.

From here we can go back to the heart and cycle through again or let the energy cloud ascend back up through our head.

What we have done here is pay some deep attention to the organ systems that work so well for us, moment to moment. We have thanked them for this wonderful work and we have instilled the positive qualities of courage, surrender, joy, free flowingness, empathy and groundedness and the will to face the changes and experiences in our life positively and creatively – certainly all valuable qualities!

Do this practice daily or whenever you feel a need to get in touch with those qualities that the organs represent. In time you will become sensitized to the health, the vitality and the inner integrity of not only your inner organs but your emotions as well.

Ancient practices, including the most secret, are now available to you. The need to travel, difficulty finding teachers, and various hardships kept the information hidden from most people not that long ago. Though today time can be difficult to set aside, it is much easier for anyone to access and begin this whole alchemical transmutational process than in historical times. It was once secret knowledge. Now, the basis of the Three Treasures and how to use them with personal daily practice is more easily available to you. If you can sort through the overload of information, you can find the truth.

You can have access to secret knowledge. It takes energy and diligence to sort through the immense body of knowledge available through global information systems. If you do the work to find a master teacher and practice with virtue, you can gain a closer link to enlightened dimensions. You can be healthier, happier, more vibrant, more blissful, more energetic, and heal yourself.

The secret of Chinese medicine is using the available methods until your qi becomes your teacher. What underlies all these inner cultivation traditions is that the qi or the energy is experienced and felt as a living tangible force and that this force has the ability to increase as you age. This force links your mind with the mind of the Universe. They have never been separate.

KEY CONCEPTS
- The essential flow of life is qi.
- Qi is the basic source of the proper flow of health in the body.
- Flow of qi associates with all parts of the body.
- Chinese medicine uses outside sources to manipulate inner channels to maximize flow of qi.
- Good health, it should be noted, is essential for enlightenment.
- Complete health, longevity, and enlightenment will be achieved by opening the energy channels of the body.

CHAPTER SEVENTEEN
What is Real Kung Fu?

Kung Fu (pronounced Gong Fu in Chinese) is a multi-layered system of energy work with highly tuned physical techniques and a hidden element of spiritual awakening. In fact, kung fu ("hard work"), like most martial arts, was often developed in religious monasteries. A not so well known, but crucial, element that underlies martial arts are the specific meditations. Kung fu also includes training the Three Treasures with diet, exercise, and by preserving reproductive energy. Chinese martial arts integrate Chinese medicine, shamanic practices, alchemy, and Taoist qi gong energy theory.

Longevity is considered an important part of these teachings. Once a person starts middle age, it is important to reduce the inflammation in the body by cooling down the internal fire. For this reason older people aren't advised to break bricks with bare hands. However, every village enjoyed the prospect of watching their own ancient master turn his wrinkled body to the newest young challenger, whipping his long white beard around to face the upstart, and generally beating him before the younger man could complete his first move.

These elderly masters knew that breathing correctly, combining breath with motion and stillness and slowing the mind all charge the body with greater amounts of qi. The ancient concept of cultivating qi in the body both for survival and for use in the martial arts stems from the understanding of how a body functions differently with less or more qi. As your qi gong master teacher guides you in correct breathing, you begin to recreate conception within your body. This involves a technique called embryonic breathing, an internal elixir qi gong. With correct breathing, you can achieve the union of the Yang Spirit and the Yin Soul, the mother and child lights. Soon, you will find your spiritual center. When you unify your spirit and the qi in your lower torso, you are capable of reaching the state of "embracing singularity." Using embryonic breathing, you can build your qi to an abundant level in your dantian, or lower abdomen. Martial arts combined with embryonic breathing are tremendous for building up qi.

Embracing singularity describes the subtle body actually embracing the Golden Embryo, which dissolves into nothingness. Chang Po Tuan describes this as a "husband and wife in blissful embrace. This is a real experience, not a metaphor." Realization results, and through realization, you experience liberation.

As in all inner alchemy methods, the focus lies in raising, cultivating, and circulating qi. High-level martial artists retain their abilities and are capable of defeating younger practitioners, even in their advanced years. In fact, at 70 or even 80 years old, the high level martial artist with highly cultivated qi can be stronger than a much younger man or woman. Similar to the Obi-Wan Kenobi or Yoda archetypes, stories abound of grandmasters who best their young opponents before they can even strike once. These masters have superhuman mental and energetic ability. They also use their knowledge of all possibilities of movement and choose the most likely, staying one step ahead of the younger adept. Their strategy has a scientific aspect because the possibilities are finite and experience and careful scrutiny of the young challenger gives the 80 year-old expert an advantage.

True masters of martial arts regulate their emotional mind with peace, harmony and calmness. They pursue the true meaning of life, and cultivate qi to raise the spirit. The bio-electricity of qi brings power to the physical body. The final goal in martial arts is to reach enlightenment. Unification of the human spirit bodies requires an abundance of stored qi. When there are vast quantities of qi, it can be used to strengthen the physical body and nourish the brain to an enlightened state. A strong physical body gives the long life needed for spiritual cultivation. When the brain is highly nourished, the third eye will be reopened and the meaning of life clearly understood.

Qi gong, kung fu, and tai chi are modern labels for collections of methods that are ancient systems of internal energy cultivation that use a variety of practices based upon activating the core energy or qi. This activation greatly enhances the consciousness and performance of both mind and body.

To change muscle and tendons in qi gong, for instance, you learn small circulation stimulation. You use your mind to lead the qi to circulate smoothly and abundantly along the two major qi vessels, the conception and governing meridians. Circulating further in all twelve primary qi channels, the qi movement is smooth and abundant. Your physical body becomes well conditioned and you glow from internal health.

Another goal in qi gong is called "brain washing grand circulation." Your qi is lead from your lower torso up through the spinal column, or thrusting vessel, to the brain to activate more brain cells and energize them to a state of higher vitality. At that point your third eye can be reopened and enlightenment can be achieved.

By manipulating the body through embryonic breathing and through the practice of qi gong one can reach enlightenment. In your body itself are the sources of your internal paths to wholeness. Qi gong is basically a practice to access, circulate and then store qi in your system. It can be used for health concerns, for building up internal strength, and for opening the inner spiritual centers of the body. These practices range from very simple natural breathing exercises to very powerful and complicated forms that can only be learned from a teacher.

Kuan-yin (the bodhisattva of compassion) surrounded by magic formulae for producing embryonic breathing

Qi gong masters assert that moving this qi energy up through the body activates latent aspects of the human brain, integrating them all in such a way as to hit a switch that completes a circuit of microcosm to macrocosm.

While the Buddha looked deep within himself to find the source of enlightenment, the Chinese looked to Nature. Using their observations about Nature, they applied the same principles to their inner lives. This power through the Web of Nature – the Tao – is the paradigm. From this paradigm arose Chinese alchemy, but that was not all. From the Web of Life, from the Tao, from the observance and applications of energies and patterns of Nature, there also arose the martial arts.

Energy Points Activated in Qi Gong Practice

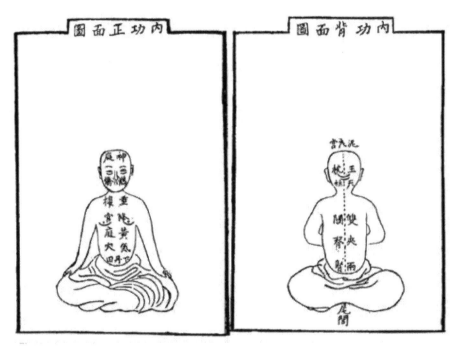

A woman performs a qi gong routine outdoors.

The unification of yin and yang energies within the body results in greatly enhanced longevity, health and perception. Qi gong practices are designed to facilitate this unification and there are both "hard" and "soft" versions, that are external or internal.

Hard style can be distinguished from soft style because it primarily strengthens the body. Weights may be used. Soft styles include the dance-like quality of tai chi or water boxing. Soft styles are credited with healing powers for even the most difficult to treat chronic illnesses, such as fibromyalgia. There is a standing method that can cause white hair to darken due to better qi circulation. Tai chi, qi gong, diet, and acupuncture all have proven restorative powers.

Tai chi chuan or "supreme ultimate fist" is also the unification of yin and yang, and the product of emptiness. Its shamanistic origin is evident in the dream story of its founder. He is said to have had a dream inhabited by a god named Kuan-ti who provided him with the necessary skills to defeat demons. Thus, Kuan-ti is the god of martial arts and tai chi is recognized as one of the primary martial arts in China.

Another version is that of Zhang San Feng, a famous Taoist Immortal, who observed a fight between a snake and a crane. The warrior monks of old practiced in hermitages on top of the five sacred mountains of Taoism. On one mountain, Wu Dang, this legendary alchemist watched an epic battle between a crane and a snake. He watched how they moved in combat, each with its own strengths. The crane aggressively attacked the serpent again and again, which moved easily out of the way with agile flowing movements before striking back. The crane moved with speed and mobility, countering perfectly. Both fought using their unique strengths and remained unharmed. He saw the aesthetics of the snake winding and unwinding and the crane stepping gracefully out of the way. He thought of qi moving and countering spontaneously with perfect integration in the flow. This was the beginning inspiration for tai chi by an enlightened master. Zhang San Feng began to imitate their movements himself and so developed a set of movements to strengthen and free up the flow of energy or qi in the body.

The Qi Gong Five Animals (Wu Qin Xi)

Strengthening the energy and vitality of the body was promoted by exercises following the natural movements and postures of five different animals introduced by Hua Tou 110-207 AD. They include the Tiger, Deer, Bear, Monkey and Crane.

174

Martial arts have been broken down into internal and external styles, which correspond to different approaches in the training method. Originally, both internal and external systems in the Taoist and Buddhist traditions were supposed to result in enlightenment.

The internal training method is based on going from inside to outside through breathing and meditation. Tai chi and qi gong are internal methods.

Tai chi is popular because of its many health benefits. Its rhythmic movements, postures, and breathing help digestion, blood pressure and circulation, and generally massage and maintain the health of all internal organs. Tai chi increases the circulation of vital energy or qi within the body, thus performing the same objective as Chinese Medicine, balancing a healthy flow of the primal energy along the meridians. The key word is gentle movement. This is why tai chi is such a popular and appropriate exercise for seniors.

The external method goes from outside to inside and emphasizes hardening the body and muscle and bone training. There are different kinds of kung fu but many external martial arts these days are acrobatic in nature. In fact, they are much closer to gymnastics than traditional martial arts, which were used to survive encounters with dangerous enemies — animal or human. Survival was connected to the amount of qi in the body. For instance, the tiger defeats a larger animal because its qi is stronger. The strongest qi is seen in the person who has achieved inner illumination. The primary goal of tai chi is inner illumination, when all the meridians are opened.

In Taoism there is the idea that spirit animals are magical and powerful and cultivate qi. Many other forms of Chinese exercises, such as the Five Animal Frolics as well as various qi gong forms such as Soaring Crane and Wild Goose, also use animal movements. The ancient Taoists were great observers of Nature and based many of their practices on what they saw and experienced there.

So the tiger, with its abundance of qi, is seen as the symbol of the warrior and maximum qi development. Many systems of martial arts have tiger movements within them. The tortoise was seen to hibernate during the cold season and come back to life after suspended animation. The long life of the turtle was admired and so is often seen as a representation of longevity. Many ancient shamanic systems were based on copying the breathing patterns of turtles, as a pattern for longevity. Tortoise breathing is an ancient method of qi cultivation. Also, each tribe or village had a personal totem animal guide which was known to appear in the form of teacher or guide to the village shaman.

Generally, the Dragon, the Snake, and the White Crane systems are more associated with qi development, or internal training as are tai chi, bagua and xingyi. The carp, with its graceful moving tail, can be a metaphor for tai chi. There are dragon metaphors in water boxing, symbolizing immortality as well as kundalini. The dragon originally came from nine different animals and each represents a different region that united under a common powerful military leader. He would have been the top martial arts master, determined by ritualized contests between generals, as well as the best swordsman.

Praying mantis movements are in both northern and southern versions. In the tai chi ideal, there is a natural respect and veneration for the animal world, flowers, and bamboo. The power and harmony of nature are seen in flowers and animals and repeated in various yoga postures.

The internal styles enable you to have the strength, suppleness, and flexibility of a baby. A two year old can drop straight down, do the splits, or squat. A baby's strength is needed to cry long and hard to be sure survival needs are met. Qi development takes you back to that original embryonic level of qi.

In Taoism, the soft overcomes the hard. In Nature, water is more powerful than stone, and often flexibility defeats strength. In fact, although muscle tone is a product of the martial arts, large muscle mass is not necessary and can even be a hindrance. Real martial arts, based on qi development, do not rely on size, strength, and youth.

Real martial arts were formed from spiritual practice and used for survival. They focused on the conjoining of soul and spirit with the body.

The ideal real kung fu master was as comfortable taking a challenge with a sword or spear as with empty hands. There were exotic weapons, but the primary ones used were staff or spear, a double edged straight sword, and a broad sword. The natural sword movements involve dexterity and alignment that are consistent with maximum qi development. Natural movements were emphasized. Legendary blades were unbreakable, magically forged. The body of the swordsman was trained to maintain a natural alignment and maximum qi development. A person with any fear or hesitation was most likely to die; a person who transcended the self and thus was not controlled by fear, uncertainty, or fatigue was able

176

to survive time after time in life or death situations.

The mastery of the sword was a metaphor for enlightenment. The sword represents the enlightened mind. It represents who you really are when you see your Original Face. You can enter the Tao by combining qi cultivation with martial arts practice.

A martial arts lineage holder received the complete system passed on from the head of the previous generation. Surviving lineages came from masters who had achieved high levels of the style. Their students were able to pass on their systems in turn. Alchemical texts also documented knowledge about these practices. In their symbolic "twilight language," different systems described inner illumination, although disguised. Often references were found to the Golden Embryo, or Elixir of Immortality.

Movements and breathing meditations in qi gong exercises are based on subtle body activation. When there is a significant increase in the oxygen carrying capacity of the circulatory system, there is an increase in qi. You center your focus on life force, the qi, which should be the anchor for awareness. This qi, when properly distributed through your body and mind, activates the connection of microcosm to macrocosm. You realize that "you" are not the massive strata of identifiers which confuse and distract. You are qi. You have the ability to unite the energy of your body with the energy of the universe. Qi runs through the universe. You are one with it, eternal and immortal.

The more seamlessly those connections are made between the concrete and the abstract, the body and the spirit, the more qi is seen as immaterial. But being immaterial doesn't exclude it from existence. And by yoking the immaterial to the material, the spirit through the mind's fusion to the body, an equilibrium and harmony is established which is centered on the bridge of vitality and meaning.

Real kung fu is the physical use of the body to infuse a life with vitality and meaning. You learn from breathing, moving and visualization exercises. Using qi, you build up energies in your body that are primarily headed for that union of yin/yang and Tao, but you also benefit from the release of physical tension and emotional stress.

The proponents of tai chi and qi gong report that gaining control of this qi flow is rather like learning to ride a bicycle or shift gears in a car with a manual transmission. Eventually, you get the feel of it. Learning this ability through the exercises of tai chi and qi gong — and if properly used, all areas of kung fu — will allow this balanced state to flow in a continuum in all the areas of life, centering that energy in a calm and natural place, rather than in radical and destructive emotions.

As Doctor Yang Jwing Ming says, "Embryonic breathing is only the first step. Once you have established a habit for your meditation, soon you will realize that you are dancing in a spiritual garden, which is hard to describe to other people."[1]

If the elements of the Tao cannot be expressed in words, as Lao Tzu suggested, how can it be expressed, used, realized? Perhaps it can be expressed in the martial arts. The martial arts activate the original essence of the mind, their disciplines harmonizing and fusing the body with this powerful and vital force of existence. This ancient warrior system, based on transcending the false self, is associated with virtue and honor and the goal of seeing your Original Face, the true self.

Any of the martial arts that are linked with realization of the Tao and leading toward the completion stage of meditation are pathways to enlightenment without the hardship of renunciation. The path of natural movement is discovered by relaxing, listening inwardly and slowing down, all of which takes you out of your conditioned mental and physical habits and allows you to drop into Tao.

Across the globe, you can imagine a powerful circuit switching on, activating the coiled up serpent power, the kundalini at the base of the spine of human knowledge. It rises up and up along the meridians and the neural networks of a new socio-cultural paradigm, to reach the collective human brain and open the pineal gland of the human collective unconscious, to activate a new consciousness.

But there is no need to wait for this revolution to fully dawn. You can feel it in yourself, practicing qi gong, tai chi or internal martial arts such as bagua or xingyi, mindful and appreciative of the process. Actually the abundance of time, methodologies and a higher standard of living at this point in all the Western countries makes it easier to have a life based on achieving greater and greater levels of inner illumination than at any other time in history.

KEY CONCEPTS
- To master embryonic breathing would be to fully recreate conception within the body – the union of the Yang Spirit and the Yin Soul, the Mother and Child lights.
- The heart of this experience is "embracing singularity" which

1 *Embryonic Breathing* by Dr. Yang, Jwing-Ming, *Inside Kung Fu*, January 14, 2008

describes the subtle body actually embracing the Golden Embryo which dissolves into emptiness – the return to Void.

- Moving qi up though the body activates latent aspects of the human brain by opening the energy meridians of the body and uniting the individual mind with the mind of the Tao.
- Embracing singularity reopens the third eye, resulting in permanent inner illumination.
- There are both internal and external martial arts and qi gong self-cultivation methods, all of which were originally focused on achieving enlightenment.

CHAPTER EIGHTEEN
Science Rediscovers The Philosopher's Stone

As Western scientists research into all parts of life, matter, energy, and consciousness, it is inevitable that they rediscover the lost secret of immortality, the veritable Philosophers Stone of antiquity. This modern discovery will forever bridge the gap between science and religion. Already evidence has been unearthed, awakening these ancient truths in this modern world.

Carl Jung was one of those scientists. When he began his study of such subjects as the *Tibetan Book of the Dead*, synchronicity, and dreams, his interests definitely took him to the fringes of his profession. As the first psychologist to study the kundalini and the Golden Flower, he looked far beyond his peers. Always the independent thinker, he was an associate of Sigmund Freud but broke away from Freud's work to create his own style of psychoanalysis, which is still practiced today.

Jung spent many years as a psychiatrist at a Swiss mental hospital. In his clinical work with psychotics and schizophrenics he began to notice that the contents of his patient's fantasies and delusions were very similar to ancient myths, yet he knew very well that these patients had never read or studied ancient mythology.

Again and again he encountered myths from disconnected lands and eras that echoed one another. Sigmund Freud, in his *Interpretation of Dreams*, wrote in 1900 that the unconscious was more or less the repository of repressed desires. Jung pointed out that there was a layer of every human mind that was a repository for the universal symbols of myth and religion. This repository he called the collective unconscious. Its contents he called archetypes.

Freud believed the unconscious was mostly the result of sexual drives. Jung thought this was too simplistic, seeing other drives at work and mirrored in all religions and cultures. Everything that could be found in the subconscious of a single human can be found in the collective unconscious. This he saw as a part of an unconscious mind, shared by a society, a people, or all humankind. It held the sum of human experience and included ideas of science, spirituality, and ethics.

His theory seems to be supported in the Gospel of Luke, Chapter 17; Verse 21, where it is stated "The Kingdom of God is within you." This truth can be revealed in your physical body where all the truths of the universe reside, from the collective unconscious to God.

This microcosm of the human body was the focus of study for classical Chinese medicine, as it was for the Philosopher's Stone of Western alchemy. Its truth rings on all levels. The Buddha resides within. It appears that science and religion have found common ground.

Modern science is beginning to reveal what ancient metaphysical quests have attempted for years. Every human can experience some state of ascendancy through work with these Eastern and Western systems in the body. Everything is a thought experiment.

In his book, *The Quantum Doctor*, the eminent theoretical physicist Amit Goswami, Ph.D. writes about his philosophy of science within consciousness, consciousness being the ground of all being. He mentions the quantum doctor, the new practitioner of medicine using quantum physics as a basis for their practice.[1] Quantum physics only makes sense when it is grounded in the primacy of consciousness. Everything, all matter, is a possibility of consciousness. Out of all possibilities, consciousness chooses all the events of human experience. Everything is a thought experiment.

He criticizes physicians who practice medicine as if they were machines treating machines, the classic mechanical worldview of Western medicine and treatment of the human body. The mechanical treatment of allopathic medicine uses chemicals, surgery, organ transplant, and energy radiation.

In his view of the new quantum doctor, conscious medicine is designed for people. It prescribes the same mechanical treatments but also taps into the domains of vitality, deeper meaning, and love. "And most important, as practitioners of conscious medicine the quantum doctors bring consciousness to their practice."

This is an idea that combines systems, and looks at the body not as a machine, but as part of a process of mind-spirit-soul, with the trikaya as the completion stage of a process.

Another contributor to the new world thinking, William James, the psychologist-author of *Varieties of Religious Experience* and the philosopher-creator of Pragmatism coined the term that is used today in regards to the change in attitude: "Plasticity ...organic matter, especially nervous tissue, seems endowed with a very extraordinary degree of plasticity" with "a structure weak enough to yield to an influence."[2] However, James was not a neurologist.

Early neurologists such as Santiago Ramon y Cajal (1913), viewed

1 *The Quantum Doctor* by Amit Goswami, Hampton Roads, 2004.

nerve paths as fixed and unchanging parts of anatomy. In 1999, the respected scientific journal *Science* printed, "We are still taught that the fully mature brain lacks the intrinsic mechanisms needed to replenish neurons and reestablish neuronal networks after acute injury or in response to the insidious loss of neurons seen in neurodegenerative diseases."

Yet other findings were observed, directing science writer, Sharon Begley to pen these words in her book, *Train Your Mind, Change Your Brain*: "A few findings suggest that brain changes can be generated by pure mental activity: Merely thinking about playing the piano leads to a measurable, physical change in the brain's motor cortex, and thinking about thoughts in certain ways can restore mental health." [3]

Patients with obsessive-compulsive disorder have changed brain activity in the area that generates their compulsive thoughts. Patients with depression have decreased over-activity in one area of the brain and increased activity in another. Positive thinking changes brain patterns. Everything is a thought experiment.

It is now accepted that a thought has the ability to alter neuronal connections in ways that effectively treats mood disorders such as major depressive disorder and generalized anxiety. Patients routinely use a paired treatment plan of medication and talk therapy, such as cognitive behavioral therapy. Thinking errors, including negativity, are challenged and replaced by practicing positive, healthy thinking.

Even physicians who still maintain a certain mechanical scientism agree that their patients should exist in equilibrium in all levels of their lives — body-mind-spirit. Balance in all things includes an active social life and connections with other people, good nutrition, healthy familial relations, healthy environment, and enjoyment of the sensory pleasures and nature. Smell the roses, feel the wind on your face, listen to early morning birdsong, watch a sunset. Be creative, be a giver and yet also be able to receive. Contribute in your own unique way. Laugh, dance, sing. Spend time in the sunshine. This is the view of a healthy person.

Western medicine has introduced powerful gifts of diagnostic and surgical innovations. Sanitary improvements resulted from the discovery of what lies under the microscope lens. Western medicine has focused on the mechanics of diseases and disabilities and injuries and as a result has added a huge compendium of information to understand and use for humankind's benefit.

Since about the 1950's, hundreds of Western scientific studies on

Hindu and Tibetan meditators have shown that deep states of meditation influence the functioning of the physical brain – the cerebellum, the cerebrum, and the brain stem.

These studies have shown that meditation positively affects the mood of an individual, improving heart and other organ functions due to stress reduction and increased endorphin secretions. Ongoing research continues to discover more positive effects of regular meditation practice on the psychological and physical health of the meditator.

To understand the rich and varied history of meditation practices and correct methods of meditation practice you need to work with a meditation teacher. Understand that to access knowledge of any kind, you must look to those who have studied and mastered the subject well.

Physicians who focus on specialties have greater knowledge and expertise in treatment in their own field of practice. Neurologists, heart surgeons, obstetricians, podiatrists, rheumatologists and orthopedic surgeons all have immense knowledge within their respective specialties. Focus has allowed great depth of knowledge, but not necessarily a sense of the reality of the whole.

Holographic reality is the exciting "new" reality that Western science continues to rediscover. The trikaya of complete enlightenment represents the ultimate form of neuro-plasticity in which the mind and brain have achieved complete evolution.

In his foreword to *Train Your Mind, Change Your Brain*, the Dalai Lama points out:

Students of the mind have long been aware that it can be transformed through training. What is exciting and new is that scientists have now shown that such mental training can also change the brain. Related to this is evidence that the brain adapts or expands in response to repeated patterns of activity so that in a real sense the brain we develop reflects the life we lead. This has far-reaching implications for the effects of habitual behavior in our lives, especially the positive potential of discipline and spiritual practice. Evidence that powerful sections of the brain, such as the visual cortex, can adapt their function in response to circumstances reveals an astonishing malleability unforeseen by earlier, more mechanistic interpretations of the brain's workings.[2]

2 *Train Your Mind, Change Your Brain: How a New Science Reveals Our Extraordinary Potential to Transform Ourselves* by Sharon Begley, Ballantine, 2008.

This new concept of neuro-plasticity of the brain explains how important intention and thought can be. It is scientific proof of the essence of spirituality. As science and religion begin to work together many new partnerships are inevitable. Each year the Dalai Lama has a conference of scientists, hoping to disseminate a kind of new paradigm of Tibetan Buddhism into the structure of the world.

Mainstream mathematicians have worked on theories that have had significant effects on the way you live your everyday life, from the way you eat, to the way you shop, to the way you entertain yourself, to the way you perceive yourself, your culture and society. Without Boolean algebra – zero and one – there would be no computer programs for instance. Mathematics and physics are inseparable. It can be argued that physics are more or less applied mathematics.

Essentially, classical physics, from Newtonian physics and its branches, all the way to Albert Einstein's work with the theories of relativity and gravity, outlines the workings of a mechanical model of the universe. Based upon that, the building blocks of the universe are atoms (a concept that goes all the way back to the time of Aristotle) and the scientifically proven cosmology of Copernicus, Galileo and Kepler. This universe can be calculated, timed and measured independent of measurers — a clockwork universe. Isaac Newton was a theist who believed in God as the Great Creator; he found the beauty and purity of God to be reflected in His creation. However, this universe ticked and tocked with or without human beings.

It even ticked and tocked without God! Removing God from the scene was an easy process for materialists.

Still, because the actual process involved in scientism (science and mathematics, with strong analysis by the philosophy of science) is unbiased, true scientists kept working, delving deeper into the very nature of time, space, matter and energy.

And as scientists peered deeper into the building blocks of atoms themselves, they were confronted with principles quite different than the mechanical theories that worked so well on certain levels.

They discovered that what mystics had been saying for thousands of years — particularly well articulated by Buddhists – seemed to be true. Far from consciousness being irrelevant to the mechanical workings of the universe, consciousness is central. Everything is a thought experiment.

In 1905 Albert Einstein published three scientific papers. One proved the reality of atoms. Another talked about the nature of light. And the last, his most famous, concerned special relativity.

These papers pretty much laid the groundwork for quantum mechanics. Einstein himself is known as the grandfather of quantum mechanics, although he never seemed quite happy to be known as such. In any case, these papers published by a 26-year-old patent office clerk overturned the physics of the day.

Newton's physics started with energy and matter. Matter was thought of as solid. Light was thought of as a wave. At the end of the nineteenth century, all the measurements weren't done, but the universe was seen as a place of solid matter and energy, with principles that could be quantified, predicted and used. Proof was in amazing mechanisms, such as trains, boats, motorcars, telegraphs, cameras, and motion pictures.

But classical physics was based upon the idea that matter is solid, and now we know that matter is indeed not solid at all. It is more space than matter, with tiny electrons zooming at a distance around a nucleus of protons and neutrons. Within atomic structure what comprises all things is mostly absolutely nothing.

Quantum mechanics studies subatomic particles. It is known first of all for its predictive power. Much of today's technology, in fact, has been based on quantum mechanics. Cell phones, nuclear power, molecular biology, computer chips, computers period — all were developed from the predictive power of quantum mechanics.

Quantum physics explains why metal conducts electricity, something unknown before. It explains what happens in stars to keep them burning. Quantum physics works. Dealing with the smallest stuff, it also deals with the most fundamental aspects of everything.

For our purposes though, quantum physics is important because of what it says about truth and reality.

Another great milestone in bridging Western science with the pragmatic and scientific view of consciousness created by Buddhism is the double-slit experiment.

Although it's mostly associated with quantum mechanics now, the double-slit experiment was first performed by an English scientist named Thomas Young about 1800. Young wanted to resolve a central question of physics. Was light a wave, like sound? Or did light consist of particles, as Newton suggested with his corpuscular theory.

With the double-slit experiment light is allowed to pass and diffract through two slits in a dark board. This produces fringes or wave-like patterns on an opposite screen.

At the time, these interference patterns seemed to define light as a wave. Thus, light was considered such until the early twentieth century when it couldn't be ignored that the evidence showed that light consisted of particles. These particles were called photons.

In essence, these photons did not behave according to the assumptions of classical physics. In fact, through experiment and advanced mathematical calculation, it was shown that light behaves paradoxically, both as a wave *and* as particles.

This works with probability waves. Before a particular particle of light can be detected along this probability wave, it exists *at every point* of the pattern produced by the double-slit experiment. *At every point.*

Mathematically, the fact that this central mystery of quantum physics—that photons, electrons, and light behave this way – makes perfect sense. Moreover, all the particles that make up this infinitesimal plane — the underlying fundament of reality – work in this way.

The closest standard interpretation of this situation is the Copenhagen Interpretation, espoused by Neil Bohr. What Bohr suggested was that the evidence created by the double-slit experiment and other ventures into the infinitesimal was actually an exercise of consciousness, or more to the point, observation. The electron that somehow acts both as a wave and a particle, and decides somehow which slit to go through to create those remarkable overlapping patterns, doesn't really exist unless you look for it. It's the probabilities that cause the wave patterns.

As soon as we look, these patterns become real. Material reality only manifests when you look at it. Again, consciousness is connected with directed awareness. Consciousness is the vibration between existence and non-existence. Everything is a thought experiment.

In other words, the core truth of an applicable Western science that has given us countless elements of progress essentially states that there is no reality unless you look for reality.

A good analogy for this is a rainbow. There's no actual rainbow in the sky. It's light refracted into a spectrum through water droplets. It's the mind of the observer that makes the rainbow seen by the observer. And different observers of the same rainbow see it differently.

Albert Einstein was disturbed by the Copenhagen Interpretation. All this business of probabilities upset him somehow.

"God does not play dice with the universe," Einstein announced.

To which Neils Bohr replied, "Stop telling God what to do!"

Schrödinger, another famous physicist, attempted to show that the Copenhagen Interpretation was faulty by creating a famous thought experiment.

This is Schrödinger's Cat. Schrödinger more or less said, suppose there's this box. Inside this box, there's a cat. There are two holes in the box, like the two slits in the two-slit experiment. An electron might go through Hole

Double-Slit Experiment

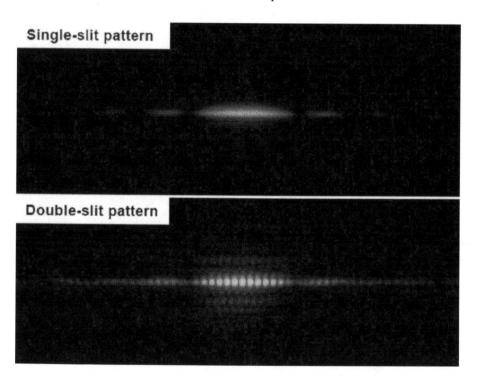

A computer simulation of the intensity pattern formed by a laser of 663 nm wavelength incident on a square aperture of 20 by 20 micrometer, visible on a screen placed 1 meter from the aperture. In reality the image measures 30 by 30 cm. – Wikipedia

A in the box or it might go through Hole B. Suppose if it goes through Hole A, it will hit a device that will trigger cyanide gas, which will kill the cat. But if it goes through Hole B, it will trigger a device that supplies food and water for the cat.

Off goes the electron, but we don't know which hole it goes through. Now, according to the Copenhagen Interpretation, the cat wouldn't be alive or dead until we lifted the box to take a look at its condition. It would exist in some sort of weird state between life and death, until it was observed.

Schrödinger meant this as an illustration of the absurdity of the Copenhagen Interpretation. In fact, the Copenhagen Interpretation has weathered this attack and more. Why?

A quantum physicist may hide himself in the math, unless he's daring enough to point out that this may well reflect the actual scientific proof concerning the true nature of reality.

As for that cat, isn't it like us? Isn't it like our consciousness itself? It's a paradox. It exists. And yet for it to be aware of itself and its true nature, it must also not exist.

Existence, The Void, One, Zero — from this pattern, the investigators of quantum mechanics have discovered remarkable things.

Essentially what quantum mechanics seems to tell us, and the Copenhagen Interpretation seems to say, is that all these particles in the realm of the very small, do not operate without an observer. They seem, in fact, to be a function of consciousness.

More to the point, scientists who are delving into quantum mechanics are discovering that the notions of these sub-atomic building blocks can't really be thought of as separate items in the scheme of reality. The opposite view, the view of classical physics and of scientism, is that things exist separate of one another, interacting, but with definable boundaries.

Quantum mechanics suggests that this outlook is flawed. Work with quantum mechanics seems to indicate that everything – light, energy, matter, time and space – are interconnected.

Once we have mastered the ways of our body, our mind and spirit will unfold like a blooming flower, nourished by the interconnected roots of reality. Reality is holistic. It is a whole. As above, so below. The universe is in a grain of sand. The science of quantum mechanics proves this on a fundamental basis.

Other experiments have been shown to prove this interconnectedness. When physicists manage to separate one of these fundamental particles, moving it across a segment of space, any kind of effect upon one part affects the other part. The laws of time and space seem to be ignored.

Quantum physics also has something to say about what we previously

188

thought of as empty space, that is, vacuum. Together with Einstein's theory of relativity, quantum physics essentially says that empty space and vacuum aren't really empty at all.

Einstein proved that matter is really just a form of energy. Quantum physics has proved that in this so-called vacuum little bits appear and disappear. Something seems to come from nothing. Indeed nothingness seems to be like some bubbling cauldron in which forms arise and disappear.

And what about the experience of the body? Is the human body frozen light which can be dissolved? The connections made between energy, light and consciousness could very well provide the basis for explaining the phenomenon known as the Rainbow Body.

Perhaps those practitioners in the completion stage of their practices, upon death, simply reduce their bodies into the light and energy, of which they are truly composed, wrap them up, and take them along with them.

We've seen that the body is a treasure trove of enlightenment. Sometimes, it would seem, upon death it can simply be transformed into light and a Rainbow Body. At the highest level the meditator totally engages every molecule of the body and with death passes on without remainder, his body dissolving into the light.

For there are worlds upon worlds of possibilities. And, perhaps, worlds upon probable worlds.

In the Copenhagen Interpretation of the double-slit experiment, when the electron is confronted with the dilemma of which slit to go through, mathematics evidently states that since there's an equal probability of it going through either, in fact, there is a split in reality itself.

It goes through both. The split results in a branching of realities. Essentially this interpretation of what quantum physics tells us states that yes, there *is* an objective universe. However, there are many universes. In fact, there are an infinite number of universes, continually branching.

In the mid twentieth century, Hugh Everett presented the many worlds interpretation of quantum mechanics, in which quantum effects spawn countless branches of the universe with different events occurring in each. He made that inference from the fundamental mathematics of quantum mechanics.

There are also other interpretations called the hidden variables theories, which say that there are things going on at a deeper level than we can imagine. David Bohm is a proponent of this interpretation.

189

He asks us to imagine a dancer on a stage. The dancer is lit by two lights, resulting in two shadows joined at her feet. Imagine then that you can't see the dancer, just the shadows. You'd see two shadows sprinting about, doing marvelous things, joined but separate. You'd think that something amazing was going on, because you couldn't see the uniting form, the dancer that created these shadows. Underlying the stuff of our universe is a principle, a dancer we can't see, a deeper reality that we can't see, so we think of things as separate that aren't.

Another interpretation has electrons going back in time.

What if, the idea goes for plot purposes, Hitler's Germany won World War II? What would have happened to the world? These literary lands are called alternate history. Science fiction historians trace these back to a Murry Leinster story in a pulp magazine entitled *Sideways in Time,* and such Science Fiction masters as H. Beam Piper, Keith Laumer, and most recently, Harry Turtledove, have excelled with stories happening in different versions of our present world. Perhaps the most familiar alternate history stories were in Star Trek. But you might say that the idea of a "what if" world went all the way back to the Ghost of Christmas Future's skeletal hand pointing to Tiny Tim's unused crutch in the bereaved Cratchit household in Charles Dickens' *Christmas Carol.*

Still, as much as the concept is with us (and who hasn't wondered what their branching worlds might have been like had they done X instead of Y) our concepts of ourselves are much more shaped by society, culture and an inherently skewed consciousness system, than by the illustrious flights of fantasy of creative media.

No matter which theory or interpretation you examine, quantum physics seems to suggest one basic truth. Underneath the fabric of the universe, there is an interconnecting pattern, like the warp and woof of threads beneath a woven rug.

In Buddhist scriptures such as the *Diamond Sutra*, the *Heart Sutra*, and the *Flower Garland Sutra*, we have proof that Buddhists have been thinking about multi-worlds for millennia. Naturally, prominent Buddhists such as the Dalai Lama are thrilled to point out how visionary scientists in the last century have been coming around, armed with the astounding tools of mathematics and thinking about possibilities, probabilities and the true nature of underlying Reality.

Buddhists, in their own thought experiments have been speculating on the likelihood of this grand scenario for a very long time.

In his book, *Parallel Worlds*, the celebrated theoretical physicist

Michio Kaku points out that it's not just math and theory and thought experiments that are shoring up evidence. There is hard data coming in from advanced instruments examining the origins of our own universe. Kaku writes eloquently of his own Buddhist childhood fascination with the stories of the *Book of Genesis* and how he found them far more interesting than Buddhist concepts of Nirvana.

What is gradually emerging from the data is a grand synthesis of these two opposing mythologies. Perhaps, scientists speculate, Genesis occurs repeatedly in a timeless ocean of Nirvana. In this new picture, our universe may be compared to a bubble floating in a much larger "ocean," with new bubbles forming all the time. According to this theory, universes, like bubbles forming in boiling water, are in continual creation, floating in a much larger arena, the Nirvana of eleven-dimensional hyperspace. A growing number of physicists suggest that our universe did indeed spring forth from a fiery cataclysm, the big bang, but that it also co-exists in an eternal ocean of other universes. If we are right, big bangs are taking place even as you read this sentence.[3]

Like the concept of neuro-plasticity, Buddhists naturally point to these discoveries and data as objective evidence for their very subjective experiences and the libraries of their lineage.

True Buddhists — as well as truly enlightened beings in general who walk amongst us and breath the same air we do – are Bodhisattvas and of necessity use what is necessary to help fellow beings out of illusion.

Was it not that greatest of Western Bodhisattvas, Jesus Christ, who, confronted with a difficult cultural situation, used parables to illustrate spiritual ideas? And it was Jesus who claimed that God's Kingdom contained *many mansions* — an "alternate universe theory."

The Many Worlds Theory is now a branch of modern physics. According to the Many Worlds Theory, for each possible outcome to an action, the world splits into a copy of itself. Like a Choose Your Own Adventure book, choices at one point in time create different endings as a result. And the person in each version is completely unaware of the other.

So, if there are other worlds beyond this reality, you can infer there are other versions of yourself. There can be versions of yourself who

3 *Parallel Worlds: A Journey Through Creation, Higher Dimensions, and the Future of the Cosmos* by Michio Kaku, Anchor Books, 2005.

made different decisions in life. There can be versions of yourself who were impacted by different events in their universes than occurred in this one. And, there can even be versions of yourself who have achieved enlightenment.

When an individual reaches an extreme level of enlightenment on this plane, it is reported that there is the phenomenon of Emanation Bodies, which is often illustrated in Tibetan art.

Suppose you are able to realize the Tao, awaken the kundalini, unite the pre-birth and post-birth qi and achieve complete inner illumination. This is the return to the source, which underlies the mystical quest.

This is the state beyond space and time. If you become one with the Absolute, it unites you with your other probable versions, enlightened and otherwise. These are the Emanation Bodies.

In other words, there may be other universes and other probable versions of yourself. But if you achieve pure enlightenment, you open your awareness up to the Absolute, you are one with your other selves.

Think of yourself as an apple on an apple tree. When you understand yourself not just as an apple, but as the tree itself, you realize that all those other apples out there on different branches are different versions of you.

A Bodhisattva, or spiritual warrior, is in contact with all these Emanation Bodies. Through opening the heart of compassion for all living beings, the Bodhisattva comes close to Tao. The Bodhisattva's vow to continue to work for the enlightenment of all beings is a clear manifestation of the desire to unselfishly work for enlightenment of all.

There are many Bodhisattvas here among us, even now. They may be great Bodhisattva scientists, politicians, and teachers who are working for the good of all or they may be humble men and women, invisible to society. These kind-hearted beings may be living right next door to you.

You can recognize them by a clear and open-hearted look that says it is not too late, even now. There are miracles waiting for you on every corner if you only have the eyes to see and the heart to feel. Begin here, in this moment, right where you are. There is no place else to go. You have all the tools you need right here in your own body. There are unseen spirits who will help and guide you on your way.

KEY CONCEPTS

- Breaking from the work of Sigmund Freud, Carl Jung explored Eastern and Western thought and created a psychology of the "collective unconscious".
- Neuro-plasticity shows that the brain is not hard-wired, and can be acted upon by thought and intention. Neuro-plasticity is empirical proof of the essence of spirituality, particularly as delineated by Taoism and Buddhism.
- The trikaya of complete enlightenment represents the ultimate form of neuro-plasticity in which the mind and brain have achieved complete evolution.
- Quantum physics, which takes reality down to a sub-atomic level, shows phenomenon that break the laws of classical physics.
- Quantum physics shows the role of 'consciousness' in the very nature of matter.
- The Rainbow Body suggests that the human body is frozen light, which can be dissolved if the highest level of meditation has been achieved.
- Many Worlds Theory is a branch of modern physics that bridges Western thought with the higher levels of Buddhist and Taoist theories of "spiritual reproduction" – Emanation Bodies that exist in different dimensions.
- A Bodhisattva is a human being on the cusp of full enlightenment who pulls back from full Nirvana in order to show other sentient beings the way.
- A Bodhisattva is in contact with his or her other Emanation Bodies in different worlds.

CHAPTER NINETEEN
In Conclusion

The Buddha is within you. You have all the tools you need right now, in your body. Your body tells you the truth. When you are hungry, your body lets you know it is time to eat. If you are thirsty, your body demands water. When cold, your body seeks clothing and shelter. When hurt, you feel pain so that you ask for healing. The truth is within you.

If you take all the alchemical traditions and combine them with Western mind/body yoga, health and wellness theory and apply them scientifically, you will end up with the framework for achieving enlightenment.

Your goals inevitably shift from achieving wealth and goods to achieving spiritual awakening, because the ultimate in wealth is the evolution of consciousness, the true goal of a successful life. The most valuable thing on earth is not diamonds, or expensive cars or castle-like homes; it is the state of consciousness at the deepest level of each human being. Your greatest treasure is found at your body's starting point, the key to fully opening enlightened consciousness. Your greatest goal is to achieve the complete evolution of consciousness, to recognize your own enlightenment. Then you will reconnect with your own immortality, achieving personal Buddhahood.

As you travel on this journey, remember that Jesus Christ taught that the Kingdom of God is in the body. He made sure his audience's bodies were in the correct state to receive and replicate his gospel. So first those who listened were fed and watered, or healed if needed.

A healthy body is necessary to discover inner truths. Your body waits to be unlocked to bring forth enlightenment to you.

But what of enlightenment to society? Is that possible? That is the most exciting prospect of all, but how can that be achieved?

The ideal teacher would be a Bodhisattva, an individual who delays the fruits of his or her own journey toward enlightenment to help others. Amongst those, a Bodhisattva scientist would be the ultimate in individual altruism, while standing in the crossroads of both worlds of science and spirituality, for the benefit of all mankind. Any scientist who cultivates qi to a high enough level will recreate his own original conception. Kundalini activation can be achieved by any scientist who follows the correct methodology.

194

This Bodhisattva scientist might be a rare human being. Although the potential resides in everyone, real Buddhahood or seeing one's Original Face, after all, is rare. The search for immortality is sometimes compared to a cow. The many who try are as numerous as hairs on a cow, but those who succeed are like the two horns.

Yet most remarkably, in the last few years the basic secrets of transmission of the kind of consciousness that can power this paradigm shift, a treasure trove of guidance, has been opened up. What was once only available through personal lineages begun in the Far East is now available simply by reading and practicing the wisdom of the many translations of ancient knowledge.

Within these translations, you will find the lost knowledge of Tibet, India, China, and Egypt, the basis of Buddhism, Jainism, and alchemy, both East and West. It is yours to find.

If you take those civilizations and their knowledge on how humans fully evolve in terms of body-mind-spirit and combine that with modern technology, modern science, modern sports medicine, health and biology, modern psychology, and anthropology you can become a super human being who has achieved superconsciousness. This is the ultimate superhero lying within. If you fully activate the kundalini, or starting point of the body, this could be you. This represents the greatest breakthrough for the entire human race in the 21st century — the integration of the Chinese, Indian and Tibetan frameworks with Western science.

Already in place, we have the Western medical system and the Chinese medical system. Now what if the Western medical system, with an improved consciousness-based structure provided by the Bodhisattva scientist, shifts its viewpoint?

The Western medical paradigm views human bodies as machines, mechanical systems that can be taken apart and put back together. This has proven to be a valuable construct. So, for instance, now we know that the brain sends messages using a combination of chemical and electrical impulses from one neuron to another, passing from one axon over a synapse to a receiving dentrite.

But there is so much more going on. Human bodies are also part of a complex matrix of interconnected factors, including mind, spirit and the energy flow of nature in general.

The Western medical system is beginning to widen its perspective using a Bodhisattvic point of view. Fields of integrative medicine and psychoneuroimmunology have sprouted and flourished, examples of the current transition in which medical experts are looking beyond the traditional Western system.

Many medical practitioners already have begun to incorporate the Chinese medicine viewpoint into their practice and use this enhanced attitude for preventative health and healing. Western doctors have begun to march across this bridge, finding value in meditation, yoga, tai chi, qi gong, sound healing, biofeedback, laughter, and positive thinking.

What the work of traditional Chinese medical practitioners, the lamas of Tibet, and select martial artists have shown us through the teacher-student, guru-apprentice lineage system, is that these methodologies can be taught to almost anyone who is willing to persevere in the training. The contents of the teachings are secret no longer.

In the West, the ideals of individual freedom encourage and, at the least, allow spiritual adventures, awakening, and exploration. You can open these wondrous treasure chests and use whichever system you want or even a fusion of beliefs and techniques to discover who you truly are. The way is open to all.

Luckily, it is no longer esoteric or difficult or forbidden to acquire these methods or experiences. Because the quality of the translations of ancient texts that discuss realization have dramatically improved since the middle of the twentieth century, more of the important sutras, scriptures and instructional guides are available now than at any other time. Moreover, there are now many more qualified teachers available to reach many more students than ever before in human history.

After a few Western scientists have spent sufficient time practicing with the best Chinese medical qi gong teachers, a tremendous paradigm shift is inevitable. Eastern and Western models will work toward full integration by all scientists as a standard, much as classical physics and chemistry are now the standard for engineering.

It shall be fully represented when Western science demonstrates an understanding of the kundalini or Spiritual Embryo. In this century, we are witnessing a period when there will be an explosion of understanding of our potential to achieve complete evolution of consciousness, which is enlightenment. This is the period of the scientific rediscovery of the Philosopher's Stone and the scientific understanding of Buddhahood, immortality, and enlightenment. Rediscovering this source of both religion and science has encouraged mainstream research in which the whole concept of what it is to be human is inevitably altered.

When the Rainbow Body is scientifically studied, for instance, it has to change the whole course of science because it demonstrates that the human body can transform into energy or light. The Rainbow Body is a known and documented miraculous phenomenon that represents an actual physiological change that can be measured and quantified, documented and recorded, and repeated. This means that it is an actual phenomenon and not just a subjective experience.

What did Einstein say? That energy and matter were equivalent.

On the negative side, there is the dark side of science, including the military advancements such as the nuclear bomb. But humankind has progressed. In this post-nuclear enlightened era the real nuclear explosion is the potential to create enlightenment, or Buddhahood, within the individual. Compassion, the concept of the Golden Rule, not doing harm to others, all these will spread throughout the world from this enlightened state.

Now that enlightenment is understood in the global language of English, the capacity for the spread of world enlightenment is possible.

However, scientific understanding is still relatively compartmentalized. When fusion occurs in scientific understanding, a great leap of creativity will cause the light to come on for all humankind. It is inevitable that some individual of great creativity will apply facts from one framework to another and a realization of the total truth will become evident. The new Western paradigm will prove scientifically valid, as has the ancient Chinese medical paradigm, which has been tested again and again by thousands of individuals over thousands of years.

Currently, the most exciting engineering project of focus is the very nature of human consciousness and unconsciousness, collective and otherwise. Such a project, though, starts with individuals. Every human consciousness that honestly enters into an intentional journey to his or her full potential, who attempts to activate his or her true self and escape the applied limitations of society, culture and ego, affects the whole.

Once one person has achieved enlightenment within a culture, it becomes available to everyone within that culture. When enough individuals have united yin and yang or the mother and child lights within themselves, the human race will be completely transformed.

Your own personal journey starts with your first practice of meditation, yoga, tai chi, qi gong, or the study of kundalini or chakras, or internal martial arts. You can join with the current flow of evolution. The pure experience of consciousness and awareness can be your awakening.

It is an awakening that affects all human society. Keeping your essence and vitality alive, you can use your body to reach levels promised by spiritual masters such as the Buddha and Jesus Christ.

Essentially, the spiritual masters of yore discovered through meditation, thought experiment, and through actual physical and psychic exploration, how consciousness works. They learned that we can ascend from our perception of day-to-day consciousness to the underlying quantum truth of consciousness by manipulating physical elements like the body.

From the classical point of view, then, human consciousness is an expression of the body. From the quantum point of view, however, the body is an expression of true consciousness. Fully activated, that consciousness can simply fold up its tent (the body) and depart into lands without suffering or attachment, in a process such as the famous science fiction writer Robert A. Heinlein called discorporation in *A Stranger in a Strange Land.* This would mean dismantling the body into pure energy.

In real life, this has happened at death in rare instances, such as Khenpo A-Chos, in Tibet. The strange story of his death, opening this journey, can be explained by the Rainbow Body, or Nirvana Without Remainder, transferring and ascending into pure energy and consciousness. Only a few accomplish this feat.

Yet we are approaching a time when this may well become a phenomenon recognized by Western science as both the completion stage of meditation and the achievement of matter, energy and consciousness unification. It could be globally acknowledged that enlightened quantum unification (quantum consciousness), is the integration of all probabilities simultaneously.

Still, perhaps the true correct course for humans to take is the one that the Buddha took, The Way of the Bodhisattva.

Above all, Western civilization must adopt a Bodhisattvic point of view, socially and culturally. Old stories tell that the person who succeeds has genuine virtue and wants to help others. This person is a real Bodhisattva or real saint, genuinely following the Golden Rule and virtuously wanting to make the world a better place by benefiting others.

Anyone who understands the existence of the multiverse would very likely be led to adopt this Bodhisattvic worldview and thus strive to employ their abilities and knowledge for everyone's benefit and no one's harm.

Enlightened scientists who have adopted this view would be among those who conscientiously use green technology to create a sustainable harmony between civilization and the natural world. Their purpose as Bodhisattva scientists would be to work for the benefit of all the multiverses and their inhabitants.

Look around you and you will see this happening now; a common element of service to others, compassion, and generosity. Altruistic people are giving away their fortunes. Eco-conscious people are promoting sustainability programs. Progress has been made in international legal systems to reduce harm to plants, animals, and children. All these progressive ideas have the common element of implementation of the Golden Rule on a social level.

The human rights movements, the animal rights movements, the emphasis on responsible stewardship of nature's precious gifts — all are compatible with a change in the collective unconscious.

The good news is that now in Western civilization, the knowledge is available and ready to be combined with Western science's rediscovery of the Philosopher's Stone.

All the systems outlined in this book are disciplines that can be taught. It is information that can be passed not just through lineages, but through the Internet; yet today hundreds of thousands practice yoga, meditation, tai chi and qi gong with no real understanding of the true importance or purpose of what they are doing. Hatha yoga, for instance, was created to strengthen the body in preparation for the rigors of the unleashing of the kundalini. Most people practice it for its relaxation and health benefits only.

A shift in understanding and purpose would surely allow further shifts away from individual interests to the collective common good.

It has been said that a soul that truly seeks, finds.

But, from all evidence, that work starts right here, right now, in this needy, needy world, a macrocosm cracking at the seams. In the next decade or two, Bodhisattva scientists will become evident in every field of medicine, with consciousness studies incorporated in the Western medical schools. Western universities already have advanced graduate programs in Eastern thought and consciousness studies. The future of science and medicine will be to enable as many people as possible to achieve enlightenment.

The good news is that you *can* change this macrocosm, this troubled world. For you are the starting point for that change, in the microcosm of your body, and the answer has always been inside of you. It is who you really are.

Bibliography

Abhayananda, S. *History of Mysticism*. 1996. Atma Books.

Alder Vera Stanley. *The Finding of the Third Eye*. 1968. Weiser Books.

Armstrong, Karen. *Buddha*. 2001. Viking Penguin.

Begley, Sharon. *Train Your Mind, Change Your Brain*. 2007. Ballantine Books.

Beinfield, Harriet & Korngold, Efrem. *Between Heaven and Earth: A Guide to Chinese Medicine*. 1991. Ballantine Books.

Campbell, Joseph. *The Masks of God*. 1962. Penguin Books.

Capra, Fritjof. *The Web of Life*. 1996. Anchor Books.

——*The Tao of Physics*. 1975. Shambhala Publications Inc.

Chang, Jolan. *The Tao of Love and Sex*. 1977. E.P.Dutton.

Chang, Stephen T. *The Tao of Sexology*. 1986. Tao Publishing.

Chia, Mantak. *Taoist Cosmic Healing*. 2003. Destiny Boooks.

Chu, Valentin. *The Yin-Yang Butterfly: Ancient Chinese Sexual Secrets for Western Lovers*. 1993. Jeremy P. Tarcher.

Chuen, Master Lam Kam. *Chi Kung: Way of Power*. 2003. Human Kinetics.

Cleary, Thomas & Aziz, Sartaz. *Twilight Goddess: Spiritual Feminism and Feminine Spirituality*. 2000. Shambhala Publications Inc.

——*The Book of Balance and Harmony*. 1989. North Point Press.

——*Vitality, Energy, Spirit: A Taoist sourcebook*. 1991. Shambhala Publications Inc.

——*The Taoist I Ching*. 1986. Shambhala Publications Inc.

——*Taoist Meditation: Methods for Cultivating a Healthy Mind and Body*. 2000. Shambhala Publications Inc.

Cohen, Kenneth. *The Way of Qigong*. 1997. Ballantine Books.

Douglas, Nik & Slinger, Jenny. *Sexual Secrets: The Alchemy of Ecstasy*. 1979. Destiny Books.

——Kaiguo, Chen & Shunchao, Zheng. *Opening the Dragon Gate: The Making of a Modern Taoist Wizard*. 1996. Charles E. Tuttle Co. Inc.

Cope, Stephen. *Yoga and the Quest for the True Self*. 1999. Bantam Books.

Cooper, J.C.. *Chinese Alchemy: The Taoist Quest for Immortality*. 1984. The Aquarian Press.

——*Yin & Yang: The Taoist Harmony of Opposites*. 1981. The Aquarian Press.

——*Taoism: The Way of the Mystic.* 1972. The Aquarian Press.

Dorjee, Pema. *The Spiritual Medicine of Tibet.* 2005. Watkins Publishing.

Drury, Nevill. *The New Age; The History of a Movement.* 2004. Thames & Hudson.

Dunas, Felice. *Passion Play.* 1997. Riverhead Books.

Eisenberg, David. *Encounters with Qi.* 1995. W.W. Norton & Company.

Feuerstein, Georg. *Tantra: The Path of Ecstasy.* 1998. Shambhala Publications Inc.

Fischer-Schreiber, Ingrid. *The Shambhala Dictionary of Taoism.* 1996. Shambhala Publications Inc.

Fowler, Jeaneane & Ewers Shifu Keith. *T'ai Chi Ch'uan: Harmonizing Taoist Belief and Practice.* 2005. Sussex Academic Press.

Fox, Matthew. *The Coming of the Cosmic Christ.* 1988. HarperSanFrancisco.

Frantzis, B.K. *Opening the Energy Gates of your Body.* 1991. North Atlantic Books.

Goswami, Amit. *The Quantum Doctor.* 2004. Hampton Roads.

Hagelin, John S. *The Physiology of Consciousness.* 1993. Maharishi International University Press.

Heng, Cheng. *The Love of Love.* 1997. Marlowe & Company.

Herne, Richard. *Magik, Shamanism & Taoism.* 2001. Llewellyn Publications.

Huang, Alfred. *The Complete I Ching.* 1998. Inner Traditions.

Huang, Chungliang Al. *Taiji.* 1989. Celestial Arts.

——*Quantum Soup.* 1991. Celestial Arts.

Huan, Zhang Yu & Rose, Ken. *A Brief History of Qi.* 2001. Paradigm Publications.

——*Who Can Ride the Dragon? An Exploration of the Cultural Roots of Traditional Chinese Medicine.* 1995. Paradigm Publications.

Jarrett, Lonny S. *Nourishing Destiny: The Inner Tradition of Chinese Medicine.*1998. Spirit Path Press.

Kaptchuck, Ted J. *The Web That Has No Weaver: Understanding Chinese Medicine.* 2000. Contemporary Books.

Katchmer, George A. *The Tao of Bioenergetics: East-West.* 1993. YMAA Publications.

Katz, Richard. *Boiling Energy.* 1982. The President and Fellows of Harvard College.

Khenpo, Nyoshul. *Natural Great Perfection.* 1998. Snow Lion Publications.

Klein, Bob. *Movements of Magic: The Spirit of T'ai Chi Ch'uan.* 1984. Newcastle Publishing Co. Inc.

Kohn, Livia. 1993. *The Taoist Experience.* State University of New York Press.

——*Daoist Mystical Philosophy: The Scripture of Western Ascension.* 2007. Three Pines Press.

——*Taoist Meditation and Longevity Techniques.* 1989. Center for Chinese Studies: The University of Michigan.

——*Seven Steps to the Tao.* 1997. Steyler Verlag-Wort Und Wrrk.

Kohn, Michael. *The Shambhala Dictionary of Buddhism and Zen.* 1991. Shambhala Publications Inc.

Kyabgon, Traleg. *The Essence of Buddhism.* 2001. Shambhala Publications Inc.

LaBerge, Stephen. *Lucid Dreaming: A Concise Guide to Awakening in Your Dreams and In Your Life.* 2004. Sounds True.

Lai, Hsi. *The Sexual Teachings of the Jade Dragon: Taoist Methods for Male Sexual Revitalization.* 2002. Inner Traditions.

——*The Sexual Teachings of the White Tigress: Secrets of the Female Taoist Masters.* 2001. Inner Traditions.

Lau, D.C. & Ames, Roger T. *Yuan Dao: Tracing Dao to Its Source.* 1998. Ballantine Books.

Levy, Howard S. & Ishihara, Akira. *The Tao of Sex.* 1989. Integral Publishing.

Lewis, Dennis. *Free Your Breath, Free Your Life.* 2004. Shambhala Publications Inc.

Liao, Waysun. *T'ai Chi Classics.* 1977. Shambhala Publications Inc.

Liu, Da. *The Tao and Chinese Culture.* 1979. Schocken Books.

Loo, Mary, *East-West Healing.* 2001. John Wiley and Son.

Lopez Jr. Donald S. *The Story of Buddhism: A Concise Guide to its History & Teachings.* 2001. HarperSanFrancisco.

MacRitchie, James. *Chi Kung: Energy for Life.* 2002. Thorsons.

McTaggart, Lynne. *The Field: The Quest for the Secret Force of the Universe.* 2001. Harper Collins.

Miller, James. *Daoism: A Short Introduction.* 2003. Oneworld Publications.

Ming-Dao, Deng. *Scholar Warrior: An Introduction to the Tao in Everyday Life.* 1990. HarperSanFrancisco.

——*Everyday Tao: Living in Balance and Harmony.* 1996. HarperSanFrancisco.

——*The Living I Ching.* 2006. HarperSanFrancisco.

Mitchell, Steven, *The Enlightened Mind.* 1991. Harper Collins.

Morgan, Diane. *The Best Guide to Eastern Philosophy & Religion.* 2001. Renaissance Books.

Mullin, Glenn H. *The Six Yogas of Naropa.* 1996. Snow Lion Publications.

Norbu, Namkhai. *The Crystal and the Way of Light.* 1986. Routledge & Kegan Paul.

Ni, Hua Ching. *The Book of Changes and the Unchanging Truth.* 1983. SevenStar Communications.

——*Nurture Your Spirits.* 1990. SevenStar Communications.

——*Mysticism: Empowering the Spirit Within.* 1992. SevenStar Communications.

——*Internal Alchemy: The Natural Way to Immortality.* 1992. SevenStar Communications.

Pert, Candace B., Ph.D. *Molecules of Emotion, The Science Behind Mind-Body Medicine.* 1997. Scribner, New York.

Porkert, Manfred & Ullmann, Dr. Christian. *Chinese Medicine As a Scientific System: It's History and Practice and How It Fits with the Medicine of the West.* 1982. Henry Holt and Company.

Pregadio, Fabrizio (editor), *The Encyclopedia of Taoism,* 2008, Routledge,

Reid, Daniel. *The Shambhala Guide to Traditional Chinese Medicine.* 1996. Shambhala Publications Inc.

——*The Tao of Detox.* 2003. Healing Arts Press.

Ricard, Matthew & Thuan, Trinh Xuan. *The Quantum and the Lotus.* 2001. Three Rivers Press.

Rinpoche, Sogyal. *The Tibetan Book of Living and Dying.* 1992. HarperSanFrancisco.

Robinet, Isabelle. *Taoist Meditation: The Mao-Shan Tradition of Great Purity.* 1993. State University of New York Press.

——*Taoism: Growth of a Religion.* 1997. Stanford University Press.

Roob, Alexander. *Alchemy and Mysticism.* 2006. Taschen.

Saso, Michael R. *Taoism and the Rite of Cosmic Renewal.* 1989. Washington State University Press.

Schipper, Kristofer. *The Taoist Body.* 1982. University of California Press.

Schmeig, Anthony L. *Watching Your Back: Chinese Martial Arts and Traditional Medicine.* 2005. University of Hawai'i Press.

Seife, Charles. *Zero: The Biography of a Dangerous Idea.* 2000. Penguin Books.

Seife, Charles. 1: *Decoding the Universe.* 2007. Penguin Books.

Shaw, Miranda. *Passionate Enlightenment: Women in Tantric Buddhism.* 1994. Princeton University Press.

Sherab, Khenchen Palden & Dongyal, Khempo, Tsewang. *Opening to Our Primordial Nature.* 2006. Snow Lion Publications.

Shou-Yu, Liang, Yang, Jwing Ming, Wu, Wen Ching. *Baguazhang: Theory and Applications.* 1994. YMAA Publication Center,

The Encyclopedia of Eastern Philosophy and Religion. 1994. Shambhala Publications Inc.

Stukeley, William. *Memoirs of Isaac Newton's Life.* 1752. Royal Society, London.

Tomio, Shifu Nagaboshi. *The Bodhisattva Warriors.* 1991. Weiser Books.

Towler, Solala. *Sacred Union.* 2011.

——*Embarking on the Way.* 1997. Abode of the Eternal Tao.

——*Tales from the Tao.* 2005. Watkins Publishing.

——*Chuang Tzu: The Inner Chapters.* 2010. Watkins Publishing

——*Cha Dao.* 2010. Singing Dragon.

Walsh, Roger. *The World of Shamanism: New Views of an Ancient Tradition.* 2007. Llewellyn Publications

Wangyal, Tenzin Rinpoche. *The Tibetan Yogas of Dream and Sleep.* 2004. Motilal Banarsidass Publishers.

Watts, Alan. *Tao: The Watercourse Way.* 1975. Pantheon Books.

Wells, Marnix. *Scholar Boxer: Chang Naishou's Theory of Internal Martial Arts and the Evolution of Taijiquan.* 2005. North Atlantic Books.

White, John. *Kundalini, Evolution and Enlightenment.* 1979. Anchor Books.

White, Michael. *Isaac Newton: The Last Sorcerer.* Addison Wesley 1997.)

Wilbur, Ken. *The Integral Vision.* 2007. Shambhala Publications Inc.

Wong, Eva. *Seven Taoist Masters: A Folk Novel of China.* 1990. Shambhala Publications Inc.

——*Cultivating Stillness: A Manual for Transforming Body and Mind.* 1992. Shambhala Publications Inc.

——*The Shambhala Guide to Taoism*. 1997. Shambhala Publications Inc.

——*Cultivating the Energy Of Life*. 1998. Shambhala Publications Inc

——*Tales of the Taoist Immortals*. 2001. Shambhala Publications Inc.

——*Holding Yin, Embracing Yang*. 2005. Shambhala Publications Inc.

____*Tales of the Dancing Dragon, Stories of the Tao*. 2007. Shambhala Publications Inc.

Wong, Kiew Kit. *The Complete Book of Zen*. 2002. Tuttle Publishing.

Wu, Baolin & Eckstein, Jessica. *Qi Gong For Total Wellness*. 2006. St. Martin's Press.

Wu, Zhongxian. *Vital Breath of the Dao*. 2006. Dragon Door Publications.

Yang, Jwing-Ming. *Qigong Meditation: Embryonic Breathing*. 2003. YMAA Publication Center.

____*Qigong Meditation: Small Circulation*. 2006. YMAA Publication Center.

Yeshe, Lama. *Introduction to Tantra: A Vision of Totality*. 1987. Wisdom Publications

Yongey, Mingyur Rinpoche with Swanson, Eric. *The Joy of Living: Unlocking the Secret and Science of Happiness*. 2007. Harmony Books.

Yu, Lu K'uang. *The Secrets of Chinese Meditation*. 1969. Samuel Weiser.

Wile, Douglas. *Art of the Bedchamber: The Chinese Sexual Yoga Classics, Including Women's Solo Meditation Texts*. 1992. State University of New York Press.

Zettersan, Chian. *Taoist Bedroom Secrets*. 2002. Lotus Press.

Resources

Taoism. The Abode of the Eternal Tao, publishers of *The Empty Vessel: The Journal of Daoist Philosophy and Practice*. www.abodetao.com.

Qi Gong. National Qigong Association. www.nqa.org.

Tibetan Buddhism. Snow Lion Publications. www.snowlionpub.com.

Made in the USA
San Bernardino, CA
30 November 2016